ECSTATIC MESSIANIC &
INTIMATE PSALMS

Sotirios Christou

Books by Sotirios Christou

The Priest & The People Of God
Revised as - Images Of Formation
Evangelism & Collaborative Ministry
The Unsearchable Riches Of Christ & Paul
Informed Worship
The Psalms - Intimacy, Doxology & Theology
Ecstatic Messianic & Intimate Psalms

First published in Great Britain by Phoenix Books.
18 Bullen Close Cambridge CB1 8YU
Tel: 01223 246349
The right of Sotirios Christou to be identified as the
author of this work has been asserted to him in
accordance with the Copyright, Designs and
Patents Acts 1988.

ACKNOWLEDGEMENTS

I am pleased to give permission to Sotirios to use my late husband's painting **Crucifixion 1** for the cover of his book.

My husband always believed that his paintings, although based on Bible stories, were nevertheless universal in their truth.

He said of his work: *'My paintings are not concerned with the surface appearance of people or things, but try to express something of the fundamental spiritual reality behind this surface appearance. I try to express in visible form the oneness and unity of this invisible power binding all things into one whole.*

I do not illustrate stories literally as I am not interested in the place or the people, but try to express what I feel is the deeper significance of each story for every individual throughout all time.'

Not long before John passed on, a book was published of fifty of his recent paintings entitled, **'The Painted Word - Paintings of John Reilly'** - which also includes the Bible passage that inspired each painting. His book can be purchased from me, Mrs Jill Reilly: Tel 01938 853612 or by e mail to jilljohnreilly@uwelub.net - Copies may also be obtained from the website Amazon Books.

PREFACE

As I so much enjoyed writing and also reading my first book on 'The Psalms - Intimacy, Doxology & Theology' - I began work on Vol 2 with the addition of a couple of new chapter headings. But, as the chapter on the 'Ecstatic Messianic Psalms' evolved, its length indicated a new title was warranted.

While I was aware that Psalm 22 could be interpreted as a prophetic Messianic Psalm about Christ relating to his crucifixion, and that one or two other psalms had quotes that also referred to Christ, I had never previously thought much about them. I found Psalm 22 - 'The Crucifixion' was considerably moving when interpreted alongside the Gospel accounts of this event. I was surprised by how much I learned through my Biblical studies about The Messianic Psalms and how little I was acquainted with them in any depth. But, Christ was not at all surprised by the content of these psalms as he understood their prophetic dimension that spoke of The Messiah - The Christ. He knew they were a testimony to him enabling him to understand his calling and identity.

There is a considerable emphasis today in contemporary worship on 'intimacy.' I am inclined to think we expect an experience of intimacy with the Lord to be relatively easy to experience in sung worship. The chapter on 'Intimate Psalms' indicates that intimacy with the Lord is forged on the anvil of our circumstances and how the Lord deals with us. On occasions as these psalms testify the Lord will test our desire for intimacy and leave us to initiate a dialogue with him and examine our theology in search of this close communion. But, at other times the Lord answers prayer and also reveals his heart as he shows he loves us and knows us more intimately than we may have ever realised.

Sotirios Christou Cambridge 2010

CONTENTS

CHAPTER ONE
ECSTATIC MESSIANIC PSALMS

CHAPTER TWO
INTIMATE PSALMS

To the glory of God and Christ – in whom are hid all the treasures of wisdom and knowledge – Colossians 2: 12.

Christ is the image of the invisible God, the first-born of all Creation: for in Christ all things were created, in heaven and on earth, visible and invisible, whether thrones or dominions or principalities or authorities – all things were created through Christ and for Christ. Christ is before all things and in Christ all things hold together. Christ is the head of the body, the church: Christ is the beginning, the first-born from the dead that in everything Christ might be pre-eminent. For in Christ all the fullness of God was pleased to dwell and through Christ to reconcile to himself all things, whether on earth or in heaven, making peace by the blood of Christ's cross. Colossians 1: 15-20.

CHAPTER ONE

ECSTATIC MESSIANIC PSALMS

INTRODUCTION

The term *Messianic Psalms* refers to those psalms that make predictions about the Messiah - his life, death, resurrection, ascension, his universal reign, his victory over his enemies and the things that concern Israel and the world that cannot take place without the Messiah. A psalm is designated *Messianic* where there is a reference to the Messiah in it and it is applied to Christ in the New Testament. Sometimes an entire psalm applies to Christ such as Psalm 22. Or a paragraph may relate to Christ as in Psalm 40: 6-10. Sometimes several verses in a psalm apply to Christ as in Psalm 69: 4, 9, 21. Or a single verse may refer to Christ as in Psalm 41: 9. There is not a unanimous consensus amongst Biblical scholars about which psalms are Messianic. Yet we can still discern that in the *Messianic Psalms* under the ecstatic inspiration of the Holy Spirit David transcended his circumstances and pointed to the person of Christ.

The perspective of Christ on the *Messianic Psalms* is also a witness to himself. Luke 24: 13-46, the record of Jesus joining two disciples on their walk to Emmaus gives us an insight into this perspective. In v 44-46 Jesus said: 'These are my words which I spoke to you, while I was still with you, that everything written about me in the law of Moses and the prophets and The Psalms must be fulfilled. Then he opened their mind to understand the Scriptures.'

God not only made David a king but made an everlasting covenant with him regarding his throne and dynasty, through whom the Messiah would come and he also let him look into the future - 2 Sam. 7: 10-17. It is important to remember that David's psalms which are considered to be *Messianic* are prophetic because they point to Christ.

O. E. Phillips says: 'The Messiah was before David's face always…and he declared him to be the coming ONE. It was the Messiah's person, power, passion and purpose that was always on the horizon of David's hope and he was permitted to look far into the future.[1] The prophecy in Isaiah 9: 6-7 confirms this promise as it speaks of the Messiah coming from the throne of David.

PSALM 2

THE ETERNAL SON

The Royal Psalms contain ceremonies and rituals for the king and Psalm 2 is the first of a number of this type. Other psalms with the subject of God's king are 18: 20: 21: 45: 72: 89: 110 and 144. The Royal Psalms were used on occasions such as a royal wedding (Psalm 45), or a time before the king entered battle (Psalm 20), or after a king won a victory (Psalm 21). Psalm 2 is a Royal Psalm but more specifically a coronation psalm for the installation of a new king. In a ceremony this involved the setting of the crown upon the new king's head and his anointing. The coronation of a king marks the accession to authority and power for the Davidic kings that was received from God.[2] Relevant to understanding Psalm 2 is its original setting. Other nations were subject to the king in Jerusalem and they would have attended the coronation of the new king. In the background there was always the possibility of political conspiracy and plotting against him that might result in rebellion.

Psalm 2 was placed near the beginning of The Psalter after the extinction of the Hebrew monarchy had been reduced to a distant memory. The anointed one in Hebrew literally means Messiah and this became a name for the ideal king of the future. It was a lingering hope that points to God's promise to act once again through a descendent of David that gave rise to a messianic aspiration. The kings of Judah had not fulfilled their office by ruling in an obedient manner to the kingship of the Lord. There came a time when there was no king, no Davidic successor, no anointed one. The psalm could be seen as prophetic pointing to a descendent of David yet to come.[3] The concept of an *'anointed one'* or *'messiah'* originally attached to an earthly king came to have eschatological and messianic overtones.[4]

The inclusion of Psalm 2 right at the beginning of The Psalter is striking. It is ecstatic, visionary and unique. 'The Psalm is effective and dramatic in its literary style…through a variety of artistic devices, the poet has created a psalm of power and elegance worthy of the drama of its theme.'[5] It differs noticeably even from the other Royal or Messianic Psalms. Gerstengerger says:

> Evaluating the whole psalm we notice a puzzling variety and combination of forms and speech patterns. Lament, wisdom and royal ceremonialism are fused into one. Above all the ideology of world dominion seems strangely out of place in any Israelite historical context, an observation that is stressed by all commentators…As a post monarchical origin is most likely for our psalm, I would designate it a MESSIANIC PSALM.[6]

J. Mays says, 'The second psalm is a poetic speech by the Messiah. It is the only place in the Old Testament that speaks of God's king, Messiah and Son in one place.'[7] Two important themes about the king are in Psalm 2. The Lord has chosen Zion as the place where the King will rule and the Lord has chosen the king as the one who will rule. This psalm also focuses on the relationship between the Kingdom of God and the kingdoms of the earth and their rulers. It raises the issue of ultimate authority and power in world history. *(As nations and their kings are mentioned in all four stanzas, this indicates it is consummately concerned with the world of politics and history, the peoples and their governments. As the psalm progresses it highlights the relation of the kingdom of heaven* and the *kingdoms of the earth*).[8] The Lord is the universal sovereign enthroned in the heavens while on earth there are nations and rulers that do not recognise or submit to his authority. His solution to this rebelliousness is a divine sovereign king who represents the Lord on earth. The king represents the reign of God in the world to whom God gives the offer and promise to make the entire nations his heritage and to rule over them. The king, the Son of God, will bring the nations from the ends of the earth into submission to the reign of God. This is an extraordinary promise as it surpasses the context of God's sovereign rule over Israel.[9]

Psalm 2 is one of the most quoted in the in the New Testament. It is comes twice in Acts, 4: 24-28, 13: 33, twice in Hebrews, 1: 5, 5: 5 and three times in Revelation, 2: 27, 12: 5 and 19: 15 and these all apply to Christ as the Messiah. The verses in Revelation indicate an eschatological relevance. There are four Messianic titles in Psalm 2: *the anointed one* - v 2: *my king* - v 6: *my Son* - v 7 and *the Lord* - v 11.[10] There are also four speeches in this psalm. A narrator speaks at the beginning and end and in between God the Father and Christ the eternal Son also speak.

In interpreting Psalm 2 and its companion Royal Psalms it is important to remember that this way of believing and speaking about the king had a specific social location where it had its meaning and function. Its subject is the relation between God and king. This psalm was used to express faith in what the Lord the God of Israel was working out through the office of the Davidic kingship. It also declares the significance of the king for other nations and rulers. The basic assertion is that the coronation of the king is a divine act, a sacred act that took place on the holy mount of Zion. God is seated and enthroned over all in the heavens and the focus shifts to God's transcendent grandeur and the king's installation in the temple - the holy hill of Zion. He is given authority and adopted as God's Son, begotten on the day of his anointing and elevated to universal dominion. The king issues the ultimatum that insurgent rulers must either submit to his authority or be annihilated.[11]

1-3   Why do the nations conspire and the peoples plot in vain? The kings of the earth set themselves, and the rulers take counsel together, against the Lord and his anointed saying: 'Let us burst their bonds asunder and cast their cords from us.'

Psalm 2 depicts a coronation ceremony that possibly took place during an annual feast to celebrate the enthronement of a king. In antiquity a change of king on the throne signalled the flare for evolutionary activity. In this context the psalm portrays a possible major rebellion against God and his anointed one. The difficulty that presents itself in interpreting it is identifying the occasions it refers to. It can be seen to portray the rebellion of nations, peoples and rulers on more than one occasion in history. It may also refer to the rebellion of the principalities and powers behind world rulers and Satan mentioned in Revelation.

The narrator's tone in reporting this rebellion is one of surprise, even astonishment, because the raging and plotting of the nations against God and his anointed one is seen to be futile when it is confronted by the power of God. 'The wicked form a conspiracy and four verbs are used to describe it: *'conspire'* - *'plot'* - *'set themselves against'* - *'take counsel together.'*...This initial voice refers to rebels and poses a rhetorical question with mixed indignation and scorn.'[12] Reading in between the lines of this international mutiny against God and his anointed one we can discern the underlying theme of the enemies of Israel. Therefore, the original use of Psalm 2 may have been to strengthen Jewish identity in a world threatened with the noise of heathen armies.

In Acts ch. 4 Peter and John were arrested and after their release they joined the other disciples. When they prayed they quoted the first verses of Psalm 2: 'Sovereign Lord who made heaven and earth and the sea and everything in them, who by the mouth of our father David, your servant, said by the Holy Spirit: 'Why did the Gentiles rage and the peoples imagine vain things? The kings of the earth set themselves in array, and the rulers were gathered together, against the Lord and his anointed'- Acts 4: 24-26.

4-9   He who sits in the heavens laughs: the Lord has them in derision. Then he will speak to them in his wrath. And terrify them in his fury saying: ''I have set my king on Zion, my holy hill.'' I will tell of the decree of the Lord: He said to me, ''You are my son today I have begotten you. Ask of me and I will make the nations your heritage, and the ends of the earth your possession. You shall break them with a rod of iron, and dash them in pieces like a potter's vessel.''

The audience addressed initially at the beginning of the psalm at the coronation of a new king is Israel. In the background is the Lord's commitment to David that one of his descendents would always rule as king and defeat Israel's enemies. From the throne room of heaven the Lord has seen the plotting of the nations recorded in v 1-3. However, their plans are put into perspective in v 4 when we learn of the Lord's response. Here the Lord laughs at the wicked and mocks their plans with his derision. (Only in this psalm and in Psalm 37 does the Lord laugh in this way). His laughter portrays his ridicule upon their plans and also his imminent judgement. The scheming of the nations is thwarted by the laughter of the Lord. It is one thing when earthly enemies laugh and deride, but it is quite another issue when the Lord's laughter targets the nations. The scale of his response is terrifying as he will unleash his anger-wrath in judgement upon them. His speech of judgement will cast a shadow of dismay over them. Centuries later Isaiah would echo the same truth of Psalm 2 concerning the Lord and the nations. Isaiah 42: 13 - 'The Lord goes forth like a mighty man, like a man of war he stirs up his fury: he cries out, he shouts aloud he shows himself mighty against his foes.' In v 6 God's declaration that he has set his king on Zion refers to the place where God established his earthly dwelling and so it is constituted a holy mountain.

Psalm 2 along with the Royal Psalms are part of a much wider literature of a similar kind. Such prayers and songs and rituals appear in the known literature of the nations of the ancient east from the Nile to Mesopotamia. There are many kinds of similarities between the royal literature of other peoples and the Royal Psalms of Israel and it is within this broader context they can be understood. This helps us to understand the language in Psalm 2 that appears harsh and bizarre as in v 9 - 'You shall break them with a rod of iron and dash them in pieces like a potter's vessel.' Their original context was not tyrannical or violent. Behind them is a ritual, known particularly from the ceremonies of Egypt as part of the procedures of the installation a king. The nations over which he claimed sovereignty would be written on clay tablets and in a symbolical ritual the king would smash those tablets with his sceptre.[13] It is also of interest to note Psalm 2 reflects more than the ancient NearEastern royal ideology. It represents the movement in which the cultural history of kingship is being translated into the history of Israel's Messiah.[14]

In v 7-9 the king is adopted as God's son and it is the son who now speaks and reports what happened at his coronation ceremony. This is seen to be reminiscent of David's election and God's promise to his heir in 2 Samuel 7: 14: 'I will be his father and he shall be my son.' A privilege of adoption is that the king and son may

request favours of God. This is something we see in 1
Kings 3: 5 when the Lord said to Solomon: 'Ask what I
shall give you?' But, the declaration, 'You are my son' -
is the key truth about Jesus' relationship to God. In the
New Testament this declaration is made on a number of
occasions. It is made by Peter about Jesus in Matt. 16: 16
- 'You are the Christ (the Messiah) the Son of the living
God.' And 'You are my son' is a title also used at Jesus'
birth - Luke 1: 35, at his baptism - Matt. 3: 17, at his
transfiguration - Mark 9: 7 and after his resurrection -
Acts 13: 33 that quotes Psalm 2: 6. Moreover, it is a title
used in Hebrews after his ascension in 1: 5 and 5: 5.

In Psalm 2 the king is prophetically called God's anointed
Son who will one day be revealed as the ruler of the
nations. 'What a dream of greatness and what a comfort
and joy for the downtrodden, suffering Jewish communities!'[15] Psalm 2 issues a warning to the nations and
takes a powerful stand against opponents. It makes
God's anointed one the principal bulwark of defence.[16]
And Psalm 2 insists on the universal significance of the
sonship of Jesus for human history.[17] Acts 4: 25-26
interprets the opposition to Jesus from Psalm 2: 1-3. And
Revelation 2: 27, 12: 5 and 19: 15 all mention Jesus
ruling the nations with a rod or iron - the future
fulfillment of Psalm 2: 9. 'The scenario of this psalm is
read as a whole as an eschatological prophecy whose
fulfillment belongs to the end of history.'[18]

10-12   Now, therefore, O kings be wise: be warned
        O rulers of the earth. Serve the Lord with fear,
        rejoice with trembling, kiss his feet, lest he be
        angry and you perish in the way: for his wrath is
        quickly kindled. Blessed are those who take refuge
        in him.

Along with the strange language of v 9, at first glance v
11-12 is also somewhat enigmatic. 'Numerous examples
from the art of the Bronze and Iron Age cultures show

representatives of subject people at the time of the accession of a king, prostrating themselves before him, touching their foreheads to the royal foot. Once again we are dealing with a ritual of the recognition of the sovereignty of a great king by a vassal peoples. The ritual is simply an enactment of the confession: 'We are your servants' which is precisely the point of the exhortation.[19]

The clear declaration concerning the son in v 8 is that he must ask God to give him the nations as his heritage. When he does so the Messiah will be given authority and power to reign over them. The messianic way the Jewish nation would interpret Psalm 2 in their history in Jesus' day, involved the hope of a king such as David who would liberate them from the Romans so that other nations would now be under their rule. There was no conceivable way they could have imagined that the Son of God, the King and Messiah depicted in Psalm 2, was going to be manifest in the form of the suffering servant portrayed in Isaiah 53 to die on the cross. This was an enigmatic, incomprehensible and unforeseen Messianic interpretation of Psalm 2. 'The establishment of the kingdom of God by Jesus marks a radically new concept of royal power from that depicted in the coronation of the Davidic king.'[20] It would only make complete sense after the death, resurrection and the ascension of Christ. Gerstenberger concurs saying: 'But the universalistic and eschatological horizon of Psalm 2 cannot be explained within the aspirations of Israel's historical monarchies.'[21] Ultimately, it predicts a theology of history to which all eventually submit to God's rule.[22]

It is somewhat puzzling as to how and when the kings and the rulers of nations in v 10-11 will be informed of the issues that concern them in Psalm 2. How will they be told of the Lord's laughter and derision? Who will bring to their attention the warning directed against them in v 11-12, to serve the Lord with reverence and bow in homage and worship at his feet? 'There is a further dimension to the N. T. use of Psalm 2 which is important for a full understanding of the messianic nature of the psalm…the language of Psalm 2 concerning the Davidic king was characterised by an ideal rather than reality: the Davidic kings never exercised world-wide dominion. But, the same objection might be lodged against the kingship of Jesus. *Theologically,* one might affirm his universal dominion, but in reality the world is still characterised by tumultuous nations and rebellious rulers. From this perspective, the kingship of Jesus is established, although the climax of his dominion remains yet a future reality. It is not surprising that the N. T. book containing many references to Psalm 2 is Revelation. This contains in the symbolic and mysterious language an anticipation of the ultimate rule and triumph of the man born to be king in the language and imagery of Psalm 2 (Rev. 1: 5, 2: 27, 4: 2, 6: 17, 12: 5, 19: 15).'[23]

PSALM 16

THE RESURRECTION

Knowing the background and context of a psalm enables us to interpret it. But, the difficulty with Psalm 16 is that there is no internal evidence about the date of its composition. Equally, the text in v. 2-4a is corrupt so the translation is difficult. On the other hand its title, 'A Miskim of David' is one of six in The Psalter and 4 of the 6 are identified in their titles with events in David's life. H. C. Leupold suggests the best setting of the psalm is those years in the life of David when he was forced to flee from Saul.[1]

1-4   Preserve me O God for in you I take refuge. I say to the Lord, 'You are my God: I have no good apart from you.' As for the saints in all the land, they are the noble in whom is all my delight. Those who choose another God multiply their sorrows: their libations of blood I will not pour out or take their names upon my lips.

Psalm 16 is a gem of a psalm as it points to a personal trust and confidence in God. But, also because it points to Christ's resurrection in v 8-11: and as we shall see this passage is quoted in the New Testament. Equally, the psalm points to David's covenant commitment to the Lord and it may have been used in the pre-exilic cult of the Covenant Festival. It is his obedience to the first two commandments in Exodus 20: 3-4 that gives him this confidence in God's care for him now and in the future. David's communion and relationship with the Lord puts the prospect of death and his future into God's hands. Knowing the Lord in his life is everything to David. And it is in relation to knowing the Lord that everything else is measured - 'the destiny of the worshipper is forever connected to God.'[2]

> The whole *(psalm)* confesses, "The Lord is my life." That is why the psalmist is confident of life. It is this focus on God, absorption in God, identity with God, the Lord who is the source of life, that gives faith a confident hold on life.[3]

Verse 1 is a plea, a prayer for protection. We can discern this was made at night when David had set time aside to be with the Lord - v 7. This was probably a habit he acquired when he was a shepherd. As he spends time with the Lord and shares his concern the Holy Spirit guides his thoughts so that Psalm 16 is the result of the Lord's counsel. David's prayer is for God to be his refuge and shelter. Refuge is an appropriate metaphor if he is in the wilderness. It is a request for God to watch over his life and keep him safe from the prospect of death possibly from his enemies. But, unlike many of David's other psalms there is no mention of his enemies and no anxious feelings or psychological vulnerability expressed because of them. As a result the psalm does not develop along the lines of a personal lament permeated with prayer for deliverance. Instead, it is positive and upbeat. It is full of ecstatic joy and confidence. And a sublime trust in his communion with the Lord. 'You are my Lord' implies that David expects him to be his refuge. He assumes that he will protect and shelter him from danger and death because of his covenant obedience. David's relationship with the Lord is even more striking when we take into account the different names used for God in v 1-2. In v 1 the word for God is translated *el*. Although this is the most common name for God its unique quality is that it defines God as *'the strong or mighty one'* - in whom the psalmist takes refuge. In v 2a the name *Jehovah* is translated as 'Lord.' This is the personal name of Israel's God, to whom David makes a personal declaration: 'You are my Lord.' Here, the third name for Lord is *Adonai* that signifies an earthly lord who is his master. So v 1-2 express David's profound trust and reliance on God as the servant of the Lord.

Psalm 16 is like an Old Testament creed or liturgy of faith in the Lord that David who was wholeheartedly committed to him prayed to claim his covenant blessing and protection. So his confidence in the Lord is twofold. His faithfulness and obedience to the Lord in turn results in God's blessing for protection and communion with him. God is mentioned 16 times in the psalm - as Jehovah four times, thou, thee or thy nine times and as El, Adonai and He once. In nine of these instances the Lord is directly addressed - 'showing that the eyes of the speaker are turned upwards towards him whom he trusts for protection counsel and guidance.'[4] In v 3-4 there is an explicit contrast between those who are faithful to the Lord - the saints and those who are faithless and follow other gods. David associates himself with the saints *(literally the holy)* and delights in them. He clearly distances himself from the faithless and identifies himself with the saints. In this way he declares his commitment in obeying the first two commandments to love the Lord.

5-11   The Lord is my chosen portion and my cup: you hold my lot. The lines have fallen for me in pleasant places: I have a wonderful inheritance. I bless the Lord who gives me counsel: in the night also my heart instructs me. I keep the Lord always before me: because he is at my right hand I shall not be moved. Therefore my heart is glad and my soul rejoices: my body also dwells secure. For you do not give me up to Sheol, or let your godly one see the pit. You show me the path of life: in your presence there is fullness of joy, in your right hand are pleasures for evermore.

We can discern that the inspiration of the Holy Spirit to write Psalm 16 had great significance for David. From v 5-11 we can assume that the future has been on his mind and the Lord has counselled his heart at night about this matter - v 7. If he is in the wilderness v 5-11 stand out in 'vivid colours against the background of David's experience as a fugitive. Every Israelite clan is *secure* in the possession of a *portion, boundary lines,* and an inheritance in the Promised Land...all this David has lost. Significantly, the history of the time records these words of his: 'They have driven me from my share in the Lord's inheritance and have said, "Go serve other gods" - 1 Sam. 26: 19.' Yet he is enabled by that very loss to declare as the tribe of Levi can declare, that the Lord himself is his portion - Deut. 18: 1-2.[5] On the other hand when David calls the Lord 'his portion and cup' and speaks of his lot, lines and heritage, he is using language found in the Book of Joshua, to describe how each tribe was allocated land in the Promised Land. This ties in with the inheritance of the Levites mentioned in Numbers 18: 20. Because unlike the other tribes of Israel who had a parcel of land assigned to them the tribe of Levi had none - instead the Lord was their portion. K. Schaefer points out the Levites' portion was not the land but the Lord and that included intimacy with God even at night. This implies the psalmist enjoyed a relationship with the Lord that transcended liturgy.[6]

As David has mediated at night and shared with the Lord his concern about the prospect of death and his inheritance in the future and prayed about them, the Lord clearly addresses these issues by guiding his thoughts - 'Death includes the loss of the divine presence and joy'[7] that he never wants to lose. The Lord reveals to him that the most precious thing in his life is his communion and relationship with the Lord. His chosen portion, his lot, the lines and his heritage are not vast tracts of land - but the Lord himself. The Lord has given himself to David in this way and he is everything that he needs. As these profound truths penetrate deep into David's heart and mind he blesses the Lord - v 7.

Verse 8 is pivotal and highlights the depth of relationship between the Lord and David. 'I keep the Lord always before me' clearly indicates he habitually spent time with the Lord probably at night. He kept the Lord before him because he always made time to be with him. And because of this closeness the Lord was at his right hand, right by his side, so he was confident of being safe and secure and of never being moved or taken out of his presence. It is quite extraordinary that he concluded not even death could separate him from the Lord. At night in response to his prayer the Lord gave him a glimpse into eternal life and eternity in communion with God.

We can imagine that the truths expressed up to this point in v 5-8 are also true for Christ. He gave up the glory of heaven his natural inheritance to come to earth in his incarnation. Consequently, the most important thing in his life was his communion and relationship with God his Father. This existed before his incarnation and before time and history and continues into eternity - for ever and ever Amen. We also know from the Gospels that Christ spent whole nights in prayer in communion with his Father. As his servant he too 'set the Lord' always before him' in order to do his will. And he was secure in the knowledge that his life was in God's hands. Christ who in his pre-existent glory was at the Father's right hand in heaven, in his incarnation knew his presence and protection during his earthly ministry. When we consider the union between Christ and the Father expressed in John's Gospel in ch. 1 and ch. 17 we can discern he was also his chosen portion. His communion and relationship with God meant everything to him, nurtured and sustained him. 'The Lord is my chosen portion and my cup' - v 5 is a powerful promise for those who serve the Lord in full-time ministry and who have sacrificed careers to serve the Lord and their future inheritance-prospects. Many years ago after having left my career to follow God's call to serve him I wrote the following lines.

> Lord you've become the intimacy
> My soul has constantly longed for.
> Through all my life's changes I see
> You're more to me than I had before.

As I served the Lord I missed the sense of belonging and closeness with former friends and also work colleagues. But, in my heart I knew the Lord was my portion and all to me that he needed to be. Now, many years later as an ordained minister, what has nurtured and sustained me through difficulties is this close communion and relationship with the Lord. Although I have struggled with many things in recent years and still have certain hopes for the future, I have seen in a fresh light that the Lord has always been and is my portion.

In Psalm 16 as the Lord has addressed David's concern about the prospect of death and his future inheritance, the Lord has powerfully revealed to him that he can be confident his life is securely in God's hands. But, more than that, he has given him a glimpse of the hope of the resurrection - v 9-10. The Lord is not only his portion in this life but after death as well. As a result David expresses the ecstatic joy that floods his heart and soul - v 9. His heart overflows with praise at the revelation that life after death means life in God's presence at his right hand. Such intimacy fills his heart with fullness of joy – v 11. Long before David, Job in the midst of all his acute suffering was also given a revelation of faith concerning the resurrection - Job 19: 25-27.

> For I know that my redeemer lives, and at last he will stand upon the earth: and after my skin has been destroyed, then from my flesh I shall see God. I myself will see him with my own eyes - I, and not another.

Psalm 16 v 8-11 are a tremendous messianic prophecy that foreshadow Christ's resurrection. They predict and testify that Christ's body was safe from decay and his soul did not stay in Sheol - the place of the dead. In the apostolic Church both Peter and Paul mention these verses in connection with Christ's resurrection. Peter exactly quotes Psalm 16: 8-11 in Acts 2: 15-28 in his sermon on the Day of Pentecost when all the disciples received the Holy Spirit. Paul in Acts 13: 30-37 also mentions the resurrection of Christ and alludes to Psalm 16: 10. Our bodies naturally decay but the remarkable truth is that Christ's body did not decay God preserved it. 'The resurrection of Christ is mentioned about one hundred and four times in the New Testament. No other fact of Scripture is verified with such meticulous care. It is the best authenticated and attested event in the history of salvation...First and last it *(the resurrection)* is the dominating testimony of the apostles.'[8] In the earliest Christian community Psalm 16 was given a messianic interpretation concerning the death and resurrection of Christ. While God did not abandon the psalmist to Sheol he also delivered Jesus from Sheol.[9] M. Wilcox captures the remarkable nature of the resurrection of Christ when in effect he says, in God's providence the words David wrote were going to apply with uncanny accuracy centuries later to his great Descendent - Christ. With hindsight the witnesses to Christ's resurrection realised that they had seen a man who when actually in the grave had not been abandoned to it.[10]

David's heart and soul rejoiced in the Lord because of the revelation he gave him of life after death in God's presence and because the Lord was always with him at his right hand. Now in v 11 he says 'in your right hand are pleasures for evermore.' The ultimate pleasure is communion with the Lord in the heavenly places in his glory and presence. With reference to Christ here the position of v 8 has been reversed. Previously God was at Christ's right hand in his incarnation on earth. Now in glory in the heavenly places Christ is at the right hand of the Father. This union of Christ with the Father is unequivocally for him the truth that 'in your presence there is fullness of joy.'

PSALM 18

SAVED FROM DEATH

1-3   I love you, O Lord, my strength. The Lord is my rock, and my fortress and my deliverer, my God, my rock in whom I take refuge, my shield and the horn of my salvation, my stronghold. I call upon the Lord, who is worthy to be praised, and I am saved from my enemies.

There is a far deeper significance in many of David's psalms that transcend his experience. Also, on occasions, his powerfully poetic language points to them being prophecies about God's anointed Son. In Psalm 18 David in an ecstatic vision inspired by the Holy Spirit records Scripture. A part of this ecstatic psalm is messianic as it especially relates to Christ. Verses 1-24 and 43-50 can be seen to particularly point to Christ. While v 25-42 can be seen to refer more specifically to David, although v 1-6 can also be applied to him. If the ecstatic element of Psalm 18 was omitted then v 1-6, 16-19 and 25-42 can stand as an independent unit referring to David. The king was God's servant and also a type of the Christ the perfect Servant. A number of virtues, qualities and happenings on earth and in heaven and in the universe mentioned in Psalm 18, could not be applied to David but can be to the Messiah - the Son of David according to the flesh. O. E. Phillips believes, 'this psalm speaks of Jesus being snatched from the jaws of death to the throne by the power of God. It also speaks of his death, resurrection, exaltation, victory and Kingdom.'[1]

'The psalmist begins his magnificent hymn of praise with a profoundly personal statement: 'I love you.' The verb is unusual but indicates an intimacy in the relationship with God which is reflected throughout the psalm.'[2] An intimacy Jesus clearly enjoyed with his Father. In Christ the Messiah we have the example of a perfect love for God. In v 1-2 we can imagine Jesus expressing his delight and love for God and his reliance upon him because God was his strength, his rock, his fortress, his deliverer, his buckler, the horn of his salvation and his high tower. A reminder that Jesus who lived in the power of the Holy Spirit and in the union of his divinity and humanity, not only expressed his perfect love for God but also his perfect reliance upon him too. 'The Hebrew word for love is used nowhere else in the Old Testament quite as it is here. The psalmist bursts out at once with his affection, even his passion, for his beloved Lord. A flood of metaphors follows, showing something of what this God means to him.'[3] We can clearly see Jesus' love for God reflected in this statement. It was his delight during his ministry to call upon God to help and strengthen him against those who opposed him - his enemies and also to save him from death. 'In the days of his flesh, Jesus offered up prayers and supplications with loud cries and tears, to him that was able to save him from death and he was heard for his godly fear' - Hebrews 2: 7.

4-15   The cords of death encompassed me, the torrents of perdition assailed me, the cords of Sheol entangled me, the snares of death confronted me. In my distress I called upon the Lord: to my God I cried for help. From his temple he heard my voice, and my cry to him reached his ears. Then the earth reeled and rocked: the foundations also of the mountains trembled and quaked because he was angry. Smoke went up from his nostrils, and devouring fire from his mouth: glowing coals flamed forth from him. He bowed the heavens and came down: thick darkness was under his feet. He rode on a cherub and flew: he came swiftly upon the wings of the wind. He made darkness his covering around him, his canopy thick clouds dark with water. Out of the brightness before him there broke through his clouds hailstones and coals of fire. The Lord also thundered in the heavens, and the Most High uttered his voice, hailstones and coals of fire. And he sent out his arrows and scattered them: he flashed forth lightnings and routed them. Then the channels of the sea were seen, and the foundations of the world were laid bare, at your rebuke O Lord, at the blast of the breath of your nostrils.

Psalm 18 like other psalms prepared Jesus the Messiah for the ultimate victory over death - the final enemy. In v 4-5 a number of metaphors portray the increasing hold and vice like grip of death on the victim. There is the image of the cords, the tentacles of death reaching out and wrapping themselves around Jesus on the cross. The torrents of perdition-death look to drown and overcome him. Torrents could also refer to the powers of darkness. Sheol the realm of death seeks to wrap itself around him too and he is faced with the snare of dying. Death, a terrifying power confronts the Messiah on the cross. Metaphor piled upon metaphor in successive images gives an indication of the grave danger Jesus faced upon the cross. When David wrote the Messianic Psalms they had an ecstatic and prophetic element inspired by the Holy Spirit as they point to Jesus. His vivid imagery does not on such occasions literally relate to himself. This is seen in v 4-5 where the snares of death and Sheol were not something David ever faced, although in his imagination he may have pictured this possibility.

In v 6-15 Jesus' salvation from death on the cross is portrayed as a cosmic drama. A Salvation that begins in God's heavenly Temple where he has heard Jesus' cry and where his authority and power is unleashed on his behalf to save him. In verses 7-15 archaic language is used that is reminiscent of the Sinai theophany where God manifested his glory and power. In v 7 the earthquake is not something David ever experienced when the Lord saved him. Equally, in v 9 a cosmic darkness was also not something the Lord used to save him. But, we can literally relate the darkness to the time Jesus was on the cross when the earthquake split the rocks on the mountain sides and sent them into the valleys below. 'And behold the curtain of the Temple was torn in two from top to bottom: and the earth shook and the rocks were split, and the tombs also were opened and many bodies of the saints who were asleep were raised' - Matthew 27: 51-54. In Psalm 18 God is portrayed as a divine warrior exercising his cosmic power over heaven and earth in order to save Jesus.

Verses 6-15 also depict God's indignation against the snares of death and Satan that threatened Jesus. We can again identify the phenomenon described in these verses were not something God ever literally unleashed to save David. The storm, the tempest, the thunder, the lightning, the fire and the roar of God's voice as he comes like a divine warrior to rescue his Son - portray the enormity of the spiritual conflict that took place during the darkness while Jesus was on the cross. God unleashed his mighty power against the principalities and powers and Satan - the enemies of God and Christ - and God routed and scattered them. While Jesus was on the cross during the darkness behind the scenes there was a cosmic battle taking place between the powers of darkness-evil and God. Verses 6-15 prophetically use archaic language to show that God summoned all his heavenly authority and power as a divine warrior in combat in the assault against the Devil to defeat him and rescue his Son from the snares of death.

16-24   He reached from on high, he took me, he drew me out of many waters. He delivered me from my strong enemy, and from those who hated me: for they were too mighty for me. They came upon me in the day of my calamity: but the Lord was my stay. He brought me into a broad place: he delivered me because he delighted in me. The Lord rewarded me according to my righteousness: according to the cleanness of my hands he recompensed me. For I have kept the ways of the Lord and have not wickedly departed from my God. For all his ordinances were before me and his statutes I did not put away from me. I was blameless before him and I kept myself from guilt. Therefore, the Lord has rewarded me according to my righteousness, according to the cleanness of my hands in his sight.

'He reached from on high, he took me and drew me out of many waters' v 16 - we can imagine Jesus saying these words with a delightful, lovely and moving tenderness about God's salvation as he was assaulted by death and Satan. I had never seen this verse in this light before. But, now with a messianic interpretation, there is something quite wonderful and moving about it as it comes from Jesus' lips. Verse 19 is just as delightful and lovely as we can imagine Jesus saying these words: 'He brought me forth into a broad place: he delivered me because he delighted in me.' I had also never seen this verse before from a messianic interpretation. It truly captures the delight and intimacy of Jesus with the Father. God took great delight in his Son and v 20-24 show why. Jesus kept God's law and was perfect and sinless. Biblical commentators struggle to see how these verses literally applied to David because of his sins. But, when we apply them to Jesus we see how readily they describe him, his character and sinlessness.

43-50   You delivered me from strife with the peoples: you made me the head of the nations: people whom I had not known served me. As soon as they heard of me they obeyed me: foreigners came cringing to me. Foreigners lost heart and came trembling out of their strongholds The Lord lives: and blessed be my rock and exalted be the God of my salvation: the God who gives me vengeance and subdues peoples under me: who delivered me from my enemies: yes, you did exalt me above my adversaries: you delivered me from men of violence. For this I will extol you O Lord among the nations, and sing praises to your name. Great triumphs he gives to his king and shows steadfast love to his anointed, to David and his descendents for ever.

These verses portray Jesus' response of worship to God for his deliverance and prophetically point to the future when Jesus will be the head of the nations and 'King of kings and Lord of lords.' A fulfillment of Zechariah 14: 9, 'And the Lord will become King over all the earth.' A reminder of Phil. 2: 10-11: 'that at the name of Jesus every knee shall bow, in heaven and on earth and under the earth and every tongue confess that Jesus Christ is Lord to the Glory of God the Father.'

PSALM 22

ABANDONED

This first exposition of Psalm 22 is about its original meaning for David. The second exposition focuses on the crucifixion of Christ. In this highly significant psalm this allows a comparison between the original meaning and the Messianic interpretation.

In Psalm 22 David's faith and walk with the Lord is stretched and tested in a new way and in the process this causes him considerable emotional and psychological distress. But, it is holy ground, as it also speaks to us about the emotional, physical, psychological and spiritual suffering of Christ on the cross. Inspired by the Holy Spirit and without knowing it, David prophetically points to the suffering of Christ. We can approach this psalm in two ways. We can view it as a Complaint Psalm, a prayer for help Christians down the centuries have made their own. Alternatively, it is seen as a prayer from Christ's lips. The first 21 verses of the psalm are a prayer of complaint voicing acute suffering, asking the Lord for help, whereas verses 22-31 are a testimony to the Lord's deliverance. Weiser says:

> The song first leads us down into the uttermost depths of suffering, a suffering which brought the worshipper to the brink of the grave and reduced him to utter despair. It then soars to the heights of a hymn of praise and thanksgiving, sung in response to the answering of the prayer…The poet who composed the psalm has the gift of describing his sufferings in words which deeply move our hearts and in figurative language which grips our imagination. His lamentation is one of the most touching in The Psalter.[1]

James Mays highlights that in Psalm 22 'the genre of lament is raised to such an extravagance and intensity of scope and dimension that it appears to exhaust the possibilities of the typical and bring it to its ultimate statement. And, just when the climate and tension of the lament is well-nigh unbearable, there is a shift to a stance in apparent contradiction to the preceding prayer. The prayer becomes a vow of testimony and praise in the midst of the great congregation. Powerful and exceptional as this psalm is in its particularity it does not abandon the typical characteristics of the lament. Form and content are an inseparable unity.'[2]

It is reassuring to know that in Scripture the Lord shares his feelings for his people and the world. He is not a God who is detached but emotionally involved. Through The Psalms the Lord invites us and indeed gives us permission to share our feelings with him. He doesn't expect us to hide or repress our emotions. Just as the Holy Spirit led David to share his feelings with the Lord in Psalm 22, in this psalm the Lord also gives us a charismatic model of how to share our feelings with him. With the help of the Holy Spirit we can have an emotional intimacy with the Lord as we share the things on our heart with him. Psalm 22 also speaks about King David's fear of his enemies that play on his mind, as Saul and his soldiers have been pursuing him on and off now for a number of years to kill him. Understandably, every now and then, fear and panic grip his heart and greatly trouble his mind. Calvin saw how this psalm outruns any experience in David's life: 'From the tenor of the whole composition it appears that David does not here refer to one persecution, but comprehends all the persecutions he suffered under Saul.'[3]

The first two thirds of Psalm 22 is like a litany of personal disaster which shows that David could not comprehend why his prayer is being ignored by God. But, unknown to him, God had a greater purpose in not answering him immediately. Unknown to David his psalm was to have a deeply significant prophetic meaning for Christ when he identified himself with it on the cross.

1-2   My God, my God, why have you forsaken me? Why are you so far from helping me, from the words of my groaning? O my God, I cry by day, but you do not answer: and at night but find no rest.

J. Goldingay astutely points out, 'The first verse contains two remarkable sentences apparently contradictory to each other. This sounds like the complaint of a man in despair, cut off and forsaken by God.

And yet in calling God twice his own God, and depositing his groanings into his bosom, he makes a very distinct confession of faith.'[4]

E. Gerstenberger in effect says, v 1-2 are a direct confrontation by the supplicant with his personal God using direct speech, question and accusation of negligence and abandonment of duty. He also describes his own incessant toil to re-establish contact with his God.[5]

It does seem surprising that David the successful warrior for whom defeat was a rare experience composed so many psalms that indicate a clear psychological weakness about his enemies. As J. Magonet observes, David is a man of extraordinary power and passion, self-confident, assured suddenly experiencing his weakness, helplessness and dependency, beset by self-doubts. He interprets the groaning of v 2 as a 'roaring' from David's mouth, a roar of anger and bewilderment.[6] Groaning, because the Lord is not being faithful as David expected him to be by answering his prayer. Bewilderment, because he feels the Lord has betrayed his trust.

Even taking into account Saul's pursuit of David and later Absalom's revolt against him it is difficult to find a time in David's life quite as traumatic as that depicted in Psalm 22. Other Biblical commentators understandably struggle to find an occasion in David's life that ties in with this psalm. But, it is reasonable to assume there was a time when he felt particularly vulnerable and speaks about his enemies using such vivid imagery. Such was the strength of his feeling about them that this prompted him to write a magnificent psalm of faith that confronts and wrestles with God's abandonment until deliverance has been secured. In v 1-21 we can see alternating themes: v 1-2, 6-9 and 12-18 describe intense life threatening suffering. Verses 3-5, 9-11 and 19-21 are prayers to God for deliverance. And v 23-31 mark a remarkable turning point in Psalm 22. This is clearly an ecstatic celebration that anticipates the gospel being proclaimed throughout the world.

Yet, the theme of David waiting for God to answer his prayer and save him from his enemies was not a new experience for him as this is also seen in other Psalms. In Psalm 13: 1-2 he says: 'How long O Lord? Will you forget me for ever? How long will you hide your face from me? How long shall I bear pain in my soul and have sorrow in my heart all the day? How long shall my enemy be exalted over me?' In Psalm 62: 1, 3 he says: 'For God alone my soul waits in silence: from him comes my salvation.' In Psalm 69: 1, 3 he says: 'Save me O God for the waters have come up to my neck. I am weary with my crying: my throat is parched. My eyes grow dim with waiting for my God.' In Psalm 86: 1, 3 he says: 'Incline your ear O Lord and answer me, for I am poor and needy. You are my God be gracious to me O Lord, for to you do I cry all the day.' In God's providence David had to learn to call on him for help and deliverance from his enemies. He also had to learn to be patient and trust the Lord's perfect timing to answer his prayer. In Psalm 40: 1-2 David testifies to God saving him from his enemies when he says: 'I waited patiently for the Lord: he inclined to me and heard my cry. He drew me up from the desolate pit out of the miry bog.'

While David knows that on occasions the Lord may not answer his prayer immediately, his tone in Psalm 22: 1-2 clearly states the Lord is taking an unusually long time to answer him on this occasion. He is perplexed and does not understand why the Lord is doing this. In God's silence, David feels he has abandoned and forgotten him and betrayed his trust in the Lord. 'My God, my God' can be seen as a reproach that makes his complaint an outright accusation.

> The succeeding lines of the psalm will make clear that we should not infer the suppliant will be satisfied if this 'Why?' question were answered. The question is rhetorical and implies:'You should not have abandoned me, and I appeal to you to come back now.' Abandonment lies in failing to act on the suppliant's behalf.[7]

In v 1-2 God is silent and has not yet answered David's prayer. He is now becoming desperate as the Lord whom he knows intimately appears to have abandoned him. Emotionally and psychologically he is feeling threatened and needs assurance that the Lord is going to help him. D. Tidball observes: 'In the moment when he needs God and seeks his comforting presence, fully expecting to receive it he is faced with the total absence of God…God neither steps in to deliver him from his affliction nor seems even to hear his prayer.

The God-forsakenness David feels is made worse by the massive tension between his belief and his experience. His theology tells him he ought not to be ignored by God at such a time as this. His experience tells him he is being deserted by God…The silence of God sometimes seems most unyielding precisely when we most urgently need him to speak to us.'[8]

The absence of God has been supplanted by the presence of David's enemies. God seems distant and his enemies feel near. Why is the Lord absent? Why is he ignoring his prayer for help? Why isn't he answering him? Perhaps there is sin in his life that has not been confessed? As he doesn't mention this anywhere in the psalm we can rule this out. We can perceive that the Lord is teaching David to trust him on a deeper level despite how he feels. He is taking him to a new level of trust even though he is silent. The Lord is also teaching David to view how he feels in the light of his character, and to remember his faith-fullness, his steadfast love and past deliverance. While David's feelings are real they may be misleading and way off beam about the silence of God.

3-5   Yet you are holy, enthroned on the praises of Israel. In you our fathers trusted: they trusted and you delivered them. To you they cried and were saved: in you they trusted and were not disappointed.

Why does David focus on the Lord's character and how does this help him? He recalls that God is reigning, enthroned on the praises of Israel. This is a reminder the Lord is sovereign and in control of his life. He remembers the Lord's past faithfulness in answering his peoples' prayers when they trusted him and were not disappointed. Three times in v 3-5 David reminds the Lord of his trustworthiness in the past to question his silence and to prompt him into action.

6-8   But I am a worm and no man: scorned by men and despised by people. All who see me mock at me, they make mouths at me, they wag their heads. He committed his cause to the Lord: let him deliver him, let Him rescue him, for He delights in him!

David began this psalm by sharing how he feels because the Lord is not answering his prayer and because he appears to have abandoned him and then he focused on God's trustworthiness in the past. Now he shares with the

Lord how he feels because of his enemies. His self-esteem has been assaulted and he has no confidence in himself. His imagination is running wild and getting things out of perspective as he imagines what people are saying about him. He feels scorned and despised. He feels humiliated and insignificant. He feels his enemies are laughing at him and ridiculing him. They taunt him and imply that God is not going to help and rescue him and this only adds to his agony of mind.

9-11   Yet you are the one who took me from my mother's womb: you kept me safe upon my mother's breasts. Upon you I was cast from my birth and since my mother bore me you have been my God. Be not far from me for trouble is near and there is none to help.

After sharing for a second time how he feels with the Lord David again focuses on God's character. He casts his mind back to when he was young to describe a fond tenderness in his relationship with him. He reminds the Lord of his past protection and how he relied on him and mentions his first experience of trust in the Lord from a young age. This is in sharp contrast as he now feels abandoned by him. The Lord's absence instead of his familiar presence has now left David feeling acutely vulnerable. Reading in between the lines he can be seen to imply: 'Are you no longer trustworthy Lord?' Reminding the Lord of his past protection he also asks him 'not to be far from him' - which directly challenges the fact the Lord has made himself distant.

12-18   Many bulls encompass me strong bulls of Basham surround me: they open wide their mouths at me like a ravening and roaring lion. I am poured out like water and all my bones are out of joint, my heart is like wax it is melted within my breast: my strength is dried up like a potsherd, and my tongue cleaves to my jaws: thou dost lay me in the jaws of death. Dogs are round about me: a company of evildoers encircle me: they have pierced my hands and feet, I can count all my bones - they stare and gloat over me: they divide my garments among them and for my raiment they cast lots.

David uses vivid animal images to describe the impact his enemies are having on him. D. Tidball says: 'Using metaphors from the animal kingdom he feels surrounded by bloodthirsty, baying beasts that will not be satisfied with anything less than his total destruction inflicted in the most terrifying way. He feels surrounded by the bulls of Basham who were well known for their size and strength. He feels mauled by lions mercilessly tearing the flesh of their prey. He feels hemmed in by dogs snarling, growling and ready to pounce and destroy their prey. 'The words' writes P. Craigie, 'evoke the abject terror of one who is powerless, but surrounded, with no avenue of escape.'[9]

In v 12-18 there is an atmosphere of mounting tension. David is now panicking as he imagines what his enemies might do if they capture him. A frightening scenario that emotionally and psychologically overwhelms him. He is now feeling desperate and exhausted as he imagines being pinned to the ground and tortured by them. He visualises a terrifying scene as they gloat over him as a prisoner. His anxiety escalates as he fears for his life, when he says: 'Thou dost lay me in the dust of death.' This suggests the Lord allowed this to happen. An alarming prospect when he thought about the Lord's past protection.

As the Lord has been silent and deaf to David's request for help and as he feels abandoned by him, he vividly describes the situation so that the Lord will help him. The prospect of what might happen to David has reached the stage where he feels desperate. His prayer for help invites the Lord to, 'be not far off' - 'hasten to my aid' - 'deliver my soul' - 'save me from the mouth of the lion.' Tidball captures David's acute spiritual dilemma that his faith has been trying to make sense of and he views this in a positive way:

> Battling with the dominant, haunting melody of trouble is the irrepressible music of trust. Terrified though he is at the mystery of God's desertion of him, he does not allow himself to lapse into unbelief. His 'restlessly searching mind'...brings the reality of his suffering into contact with another reality - the reality of his covenant God.[10]

David's enemies were his Achilles' heel and his psychological weakness. In around 37 of his psalms enemies are the subject of his prayer for help. A look at two of these psalms enables us to see the extent of his psychological fear. Psalm 31: 11-13: 'I am a reproach among all my enemies but especially among my neighbours, and am repulsive to my acquaintances: those who see me outside flee from me. I am forgotten like a dead man out of mind: I am like a broken vessel. For I hear the slander of many: fear is on every side: while they take counsel against me, they scheme to take away my life.' Psalm 55: 2-6: 'I am overcome by trouble. I am distraught by the noise of the enemy because of the oppression of the wicked. For they bring trouble upon me and in anger they cherish enmity against me. My heart is in anguish within me, the terrors of death have fallen upon me. Fear and trembling come upon me and horror overwhelms me. And I say, 'O that I had wings like a dove! I would fly away and be at rest.'

19-21   But thou O Lord be not far off! O thou my help hasten to my aid! Deliver my soul from the sword, my darling from the power of the dog! Save me from the mouth of the lion, my afflicted soul from the horns of the wild oxen. You have heard me!

These verses are the climax of the first part of Psalm 22. They mark a transition that has been gradually happening throughout the psalm as David poured out his complaint alongside his prayer. Up until Now David has addressed 'God' now for the first time he appeals to the 'Lord.' There are four distinct requests in v 19-21. The first is the reversal of David's experience in v 1. His request is for the Lord to manifest the closeness of his presence. The second is for the Lord to act quickly in arriving and helping him - an echo of his request in v 11. The third and fourth are specific requests for rescue from his enemies. 'The verb "save me" in v 21 literally means "you have heard" and indicates in some way the Lord confirmed to David that at long last he has responded to his request for help. The mood of acute desperation, helplessness and panic has suddenly and unexpectedly dissipated as he was praying once again for help. 'The Hebrew vividly reveals the lightning change in his mood.'[11]

As we read in between the lines of Psalm 22, clearly, David has been waiting for an unusually long time for the Lord to answer his prayer, that accounts for the tone of v 1. 'The transition from tears to joy is sudden and without apparent cause.'[12] It is puzzling and an anti-climax that David gives no explanation of how the Lord rescued him from his desperate situation of facing near death. Was he literally saved from his enemies? Or, was he saved from the acute paranoid reaction to them. So vivid is the imagery in Psalm 22 and so heightened is David's descriptive imagination of his enemies it is plausible to assume the threat was a real one. If not he is suffering a severe panic attack of paranoia about his enemies. Clearly, only David and the Lord know which it was. But, as is typical of David he goes from an extreme tone of acute desperation to one of an exultant and remarkable note of praise, testimony and worship. And we are left completely stunned and speechless by this reversal.

22-31: I will tell of your name to my brethren: in the midst of the great congregation I will praise you: You who fear the Lord praise him! All you sons of Jacob glorify him, and stand in awe of him, all of you sons of Israel! For he has not despised or abhorred the affliction of the afflicted: and he has not hidden his face from him, but he has heard, when he cried to him. From you comes my praise in the great congregation: my vows I will pay before those who fear him. The afflicted shall eat and be satisfied: those who seek him shall praise the Lord! May your hearts live for ever! All the ends of the earth shall remember and turn to the Lord: and all the families of the nations shall worship before him. For dominion belongs to the Lord, and he rules over the nations. Yes to him shall all the proud of the earth bow down: before him shall bow all who go down to the dust, and he who cannot keep himself alive. Posterity shall serve him: men shall tell of the Lord to the coming generation and proclaim his deliverance to a people yet unborn, that he has done this.

Verses 22-31 mark a turning point not only in Psalm 22 but also in how David feels. In hindsight, he can see that the Lord is faithful and trustworthy even when he is silent. Even when the Lord is not answering his prayer in the way he anticipated, expected or wanted. The danger he was in is now past and resolved although we are not told how. This is frustrating because his sense of desperation was palpable. And we do not know if he was getting paranoid and exaggerating. The Lord has answered his prayer but we do not know if he has rescued him from his enemies, or merely resolved how he was feeling because of them. Either way having been saved his heart is full of praise. Weiser says:

> The darkness which filled the worshipper's soul has vanished and rejoicing with great joy he begins to sing a song of thanksgiving. He has become assured his prayer has been answered and that God has helped him...Having been delivered by God the psalmist is so fully conscious of his happiness which has been brought about by the re-

establishment of his communion with God that even the fact that he is now able to give thanks to God is accepted by him as a gift from God's hands. As a visible sign of his gratitude he will pay a votive offering in the midst of the godly ones and invite the poor to a meal so that they may share his happiness.[13]

David wrote Psalm 22 when he was feeling abandoned by the Lord and felt isolated as an individual. But, he ends it by placing himself firmly in the worshipping community of God's people. We have a striking shift of scene as he wants to testify to the Lord's deliverance in the midst of the great congregation. Presumably, to fulfil a vow he made to the Lord as he called on him to answer his prayer. This part of the psalm moves from prayer to praise and the setting indicated by the language is the service of thanksgiving in which a person goes to the sanctuary to sing a song of praise and thanksgiving to the Lord. He goes with those who rejoice at his salvation and restoration, makes his vows and provides a sacrificial meal for them. This contrasts sharply with his previous state of abandonment and ridicule.

In the closing verses of Psalm 22 David is so grateful and relieved for being rescued from his enemies that he is now bursting with thanksgiving. He is elated and wants to testify to God's goodness. His audience is now not only the great assembly of God's people but nations and generations not yet born. 'With an elegant sense of style, David describes a community of worship in which Israelites are complemented by Gentiles, the poor by the rich and the dead by the yet unborn. Distinctive in this psalm is the way David sees in his own rescue a glimpse in the way God delivers others, beginning with Israel's faithful and poor but finally including everyone.'[14]

As we reflect on this extraordinary psalm we are struck by the fact that after the Lord has answered his prayer, David did not question the reason why, or wonder why the Lord deliberately delayed his answer. Seeing that he quite vocally expressed his dismay at the Lord's timing in answering his prayer, we may well express some surprise that there is no theological reflection on David's part as to why the Lord did this. It almost seems as if he is in the Lord's hands for him to do as he wishes without the Lord explaining his action to him. Moreover, right at the beginning of Psalm 22 David does not understand why the Lord is ignoring his prayer, nor why he is not answering him. So too at the end of it he is no nearer to understanding why this happened.

We may see a parallel in Christ's experience on the cross when he cried out, 'My God, My God, why have you forsaken me?' - this implies that Christ had not expected to be abandoned by his Father. But, just as God had a far greater purpose in mind for not answering David immediately and inspiring him to compose this prophetic psalm, that in a remarkably accurate way describes Christ suffering on the cross, to which Christ alluded - so too God had a far greater purpose in abandoning Christ on the cross that involved our salvation. And possibly at certain times in our lives we too might never comprehend why the Lord delayed answering our prayers, nor understand what this accomplished. Psalm 22 can also act as a model for those who suffer, as Christ's suffering on the cross can give a fresh perspective about it.

PSALM 22

THE CRUCIFIXION
Before his crucifixion Jesus was scourged - whipped. Having seen Mel Gibson's 'The Passion Of The Christ' one cannot be certain how accurate the scene where Jesus is scourged is. In the film this involved being beaten with

canes until Jesus could no longer stand. Then when he did stand up he was beaten even more brutally with leather whips with flails with barbs on the end that tore out the victim's flesh. This scene was clearly prolonged and it seemed very unlikely anyone could have survived this double beating that was portrayed as truly violent and horrific. What also stood out was the brutality and cruelty of the soldiers who scourged Jesus. One can imagine the victim being completely exhausted by the scourging and it would have been no surprise if they lost consciousness or died if it was as brutal as Mel Gibson's portrayal. But, it is a reminder from Matt. 27: 26 that Jesus was scourged before he was crucified. He was also subject to a fair amount of violence by the soldiers who spat at him and hit him with their fists as their prisoner. Jesus also had a plaited crown of thorns placed on his head - Matt. 27: 29. These events alone must have caused violent physical suffering for Jesus and weakened him considerably too. Surprisingly, in Mel Gibson's film, arguably the most brutal scene was the scourging and then forcing Jesus to carry his own cross to Golgotha.

Death by crucifixion usually came slowly and involved nailing and tying the wrists by rope to the crossbeam as nails on their own could not support the body weight of a victim. The nails-iron spikes were 5-7 inches long. Exposure, disease, hunger, shock and exhaustion were the immediate causes of death. The cramped position of the body caused fearful tortures and ultimately paralysis. As a result the victims were likely to drift in and out of consciousness. Before the nailing a mixture of vinegar, gall and myrrh was offered to alleviate some suffering. Wooden planks were usually fastened to the vertical stake as a footrest or seat that allowed the victim to rest his weight and lift himself up for a breath. This prolonged the suffering and delayed death for up to three days. Unsupported, the victim would hang from nail-pierced wrists, severely restricting breathing and circulation. This excruciating ordeal led to exhaustion, suffocation, brain death and heart failure. As a result the victim could not push up to breathe and would quickly suffocate. At times mercy was shown by breaking the victim's legs causing death to come quickly. This indicates the crosses were probably fairly close to ground level. Crucifixion was one of the most painful and disgraceful methods of capitol punishment. Victims were usually beaten and tortured and then forced to carry their own cross to the crucifixion site.

David wrote Psalm 22 about 1000 years before Christ and it is remarkably accurate about the suffering of Christ on the cross. The title of Psalm 22 'The Hind of the Dawn' has particular significance for Christ. It is of interest to note that the ancient synagogue took this title as a name for the Shekinah (glory of God) and as a symbol of the dawning redemption and applied it to the morning sacrifice. According to the traditional definition it refers to the 'early light preceding the dawn of the morning, whose rays are likened to the horns of a hind.' In Mosaic law Christ as the sinless sacrifice is symbolised most prominently by the lamb slain and offered on the altar. But, in the poetical books Christ is compared to the Hind of the Dawn that is generally seen in the morning tripping along in the forest glades, licking the dew. It is one of the most beautiful creatures but it is also one of the most defenceless. It has many natural enemies and its only means of survival are a keen sense of smell and speed in flight. This is the beautiful figure used of our Lord in Psalm 22 that mentions a number of animals that are enemies of the 'Hind of the Dawn.'[1] It is also possible that David used the image of the Hind as an expression of hope that help would arrive early in the morning when prayer and praise is offered.[2]

Psalm 22 is a description of an execution, particularly of a crucifixion. Crucifixion was only practised many centuries after David so it is a picture of the suffering of

Christ on the cross. Therefore, it is prophetic and entirely Messianic. This is undoubtedly a psalm Jesus thought about as he hung upon the cross especially during the great darkness that came over the land at noon which lasted until three o'clock. This was the time each day when the lamb was brought into the Temple. 'Behold the lamb of God who takes away the sin of the world - John 1: 29. God allowed Jesus who was sinless to experience sin and know what it was like to be a sinner cut off from God - 'Christ became sin who knew no sin'- 2 Cor. 5: 21.

1-3   My God, my God, why have you forsaken me? Why are you so far from helping me, from the words of my groaning? O my God, I cry by day, but you do not answer: and at night but find no rest.

At his crucifixion when Christ felt completely abandoned by his Father he instinctively turned to this psalm to voice his sense of dereliction. Jesus' cry on the cross: *'Eloi, Eloi, lema sabachthani'* (Matt. 27: 46, Mark 15: 34) is a direct quote of Psalm 22: 1. (Aramaic was the first language for most Jews living in Palestine and had been since the Babylonian exile. Many would also have spoken Greek, which was the language of the Greco-Roman empire and spoken by Gentiles and most of the Diaspora too, hence the gospels being written in Greek). Mays points out that, 'Citing the first words of a text was in the tradition of the time a way of identifying with an entire passage. The very experience of the psalmist becomes a commentary on Jesus' passion on the cross. In the intellectual world of Judaism one of the most important ways of understanding the meaning of present experience, was to make sense of the contemporary by perceiving and describing it in terms of an established tradition.'[3] Therefore, Christians down the centuries have seen the special significance of this psalm in relation to Christ.

Towards the end of the period of darkness shortly before he died Jesus said 'I am thirsty' - John 19: 28 and was given wine vinegar on a sponge, almost certainly a quote from Psalm 69: 21. At the end of the period of darkness Jesus called out: 'It is finished' - John 19: 30 which is a quote from the last verse of Psalm 22. In our text that verse reads, 'he has done it' referring to God as the subject. But there is no object for the verb in Hebrew, and it can equally well translated: 'It is finished.[4] Bruner says, 'As there was a unique fellowship with God in his life and preaching, so in Christ's death there was a unique abandonment by God.'[5]

Amos 8: 9a-10b reads: 'And on that day' says the Lord God, 'I will make the sun go down at noon, and darken the earth in broad daylight. I will make it like the mourning for an only son.' This is a reminder we do well to remember the impact of Christ's crucifixion on God the Father. The darkness can be seen to be symbolic portraying God's mourning and suffering too. As Bruner says 'The most portentous thing ever to happen is happening now.'[6] The language of darkness is symbolic of the darkness that passes over the face of God and in the heavenly places and perhaps also symbolises a cosmic sadness as its Creator dies. The darkness can also represent the wrath of God as Christ the 'lamb of God' - John 1: 35 takes away the sin of the world. Darkness can also point in the narrative to the activity of the evil one against Jesus. The darkness was when Jesus was arrested - Luke 22: 53. It can also symbolise the activity of the powers of darkness against Jesus on the cross. But, the darkness gives way to light and the victory of God over the principalities and powers that God disarmed and made a public example of by triumphing over them in Christ on the cross - Colossians 1: 15.

J. Moltmann says, 'the Son suffers and dies on the cross. The Father suffers with him...The Christ event on the cross is a God event. And conversely the God event takes place on the cross of the risen Christ. Here God has not just acted externally in his unattainable glory and eternity. Here he has acted in himself and gone on to suffering himself...Christology must take seriously the fact that God himself really enters into the suffering of his Son and in so doing is and remains completely God.[7] Jesus has undeniably suffered on the cross, but, God his Father has also suffered as he has abandoned his Son who became an offering-sacrifice for the sin of the world. A rupture occurred in their relationship in the Trinity for the first and last time. God feels the pain of separation from Jesus in a profound way too, as his Son suffers not only emotionally and physically but also spiritually as he experiences sin in his life. In some measure the Father shares in Jesus' suffering. For God and Christ had been inseparable before time and history as Jesus had always been in the bosom of the Father - John 1: 18. Their divine union and communion was ruptured. It was heartbreaking.

From v 1-2 we can imagine that on the cross Christ prayed to be saved by God and that he cried out in a loud voice. In v 2 the literal Hebrew translation for cry is 'roaring.' This implies an emotional and physical agony, loudly imploring God in excruciating pain to help and save him. Instead of being strengthened and comforted by God's presence Christ felt his father's absence. Verse 1 poignantly captures Christ's sense of dereliction when he felt completely abandoned by his Father. On the cross a rupture occurred in the Trinity between God and Christ as he was abandoned by the Father and separated from him. Christ was cut off from his relationship with the Father for the first time. As he quoted Psalm 22: 1 and asked 'Why?' - perhaps, it was the shock of separation he had not anticipated. For Jesus who had been in the 'bosom of the Father' before time and history this was unbearably traumatic. Perhaps, he was expecting God to intervene on the cross and save him. Perhaps, it was during these last three hours on the cross Jesus fully grasped his death was essential for the forgiveness of sins and the reason for his abandonment.

The first two thirds of Psalm 22 is like a litany of personal disaster which shows that David could not comprehend why his prayer is being ignored by God. But, unknown to him, God had a greater purpose in not answering him immediately. Unknown to David his psalm was to have a deeply significant prophetic meaning for Christ as he identified himself with it on the cross. Christians down the centuries have also seen the special significance of this psalm in relation to Christ. For Christ to feel abandoned and forsaken by God most probably involved despair, utter desolation and doubt. Despair as he felt alone, betrayed and frightened. In that fully human moment he may well have doubted what was happening to him was God's will.[8] D. Coggan, a former Archbishop of Canterbury, captures the essence of v 1 that he describes as: 'The agony of doubt.'

> Now at the end of Jesus' ministry, when doubt and darkness assailed him with a force he had never known before, his mind reverted to Scripture - and in that Scripture he found words which seemed to express his need...Jesus was carrying a load the like of which none of us will ever be called upon to bear. 'He carried our sins in his own person on the tree' - 1 Peter 2: 24. It was a crushing load that blotted out for Jesus the consciousness of the presence of the God who had meant more to him all his life, than anyone or anything else. A sense of sheer, stark dereliction swept over him. If the cross is the place where God's disgust with sin and his burning love for humankind meet in terrible expression: if God in Christ is there clearing up the mess made by a rebel race, can we wonder that there is a mystery? We can dare to look - and adore?[9]

F. D. Bruner points out it is significant that Jesus does not call out 'My Father.' His abandonment has raised a doubt about God himself. This is the deepest darkness of all. Jesus is not only surrounded by outward darkness (Matt. 27: 45) he does not inwardly feel God's presence at all...Jesus' lifeline had been cut. He dies here before he dies. This is Jesus' descent into hell. We should simply stand back in silence before this awful verb (abandoned) and wonder what it means. Death is the ultimate abandonment for Christ who had always existed.

> Jesus who represents all men, feels himself deserted by God, and he allows himself to experience annihilation, this total suffering.[10]

'The God who is felt not to be there is addressed by Jesus - 'You'! There is something wonderful in that...The God whose presence Jesus does not experience, Jesus invokes. The Cry of Dereliction looks like a cry of despair at first, like a temporary loss of faith, as if Jesus and God were no longer close. Yet Jesus right here, better than perhaps anywhere else, teaches us exactly what faith at its deepest level is: it is believing God even when we do not feel him.'[11]

6-9   But I am a worm and no man: scorned by men and despised by people. All who see me mock at me, they make mouths at me, they wag their heads. He committed his cause to the Lord: let Him deliver him, let Him rescue him, for He delights in him!

As we remember from Matthew's Gospel (ch 27: 39-44) the taunts of those who saw the crucifixion of Jesus we see how closely it resembles Psalm 22: 6-8. 'And those who passed by derided Jesus, wagging their heads and saying: "You who would destroy the temple and build it in three days, save yourself! If you are the Son of God, come down from the cross" So also the chief priests with the scribes and elders, mocked him saying: 'He saved others: he cannot save himself. He is the king of Israel, let him come down now from the cross, and we will believe in him. He trusts in God: let God deliver him, if he desires: for he said: 'I am the Son of God.'' And the robbers who were crucified with Jesus also reviled him in the same way.' The physical agony and torture of the cross was exacerbated by these contemptuous and cruel taunts that sought to ridicule Jesus. Their taunts raise issues of great significance: 'If you are the Son of God?' - 'He trusts in God let him deliver him, for he delights in him' – 'if you are the Son of God?' is no accidental comment. It is the identical taunt with which the devil tempted Jesus in the wilderness before his public ministry began. 'If' raises an element of doubt on the cross about Jesus' identify that is undoubtedly greater at the end of Jesus' ministry. 'If' God delights in him also raises another element of doubt. Was God displeased with Jesus? Did he not delight in him?

> But the sharpest sting comes in the last clause 'if he likes him'…If Yahweh does delight in the suppliant then deliverance will follow. But, he can no longer have conviction about that having been abandoned by Yahweh. The mockers' sarcastic affirmation implying that Yahweh does not like him, corresponds to the suppliant's fear.[12]

At his crucifixion Jesus was abandoned by all of his disciples except his mother, her sister, Mary Magdalene and the disciple he loved. 'Jesus was humiliated, less than human and of no significance compared to that of a worm. The bystanders at his crucifixion would have seen him in this light. But, there is another interpretation of the Hebrew tolaath - worm. This appears 31 times in the Old Testament and is often translated 'scarlet' or 'crimson.' The word applies especially to the coccus from which the scarlet dye of the Tabernacle was obtained by its death. The word is used in Isaiah 1: 18 for the colour of sin - 'though your sins are like scarlet, they shall be white as snow' says the Lord. The tola of the orient is a little worm that feeds on certain cactus. These are beaten until the tola fall into a basin and then they crush the little insects and the blood is the brilliant crimson dye that makes bright Mexican garments. In Palestine and Syria they use the tola in the same way and it makes the beautiful permanent scarlet dye of the orient. Solomon is said to have clothed the maidens of Israel in scarlet. Daniel was to be clothed in scarlet by Belshazzar. The word 'scarlet' is literally 'the splendour of the worm.' Now, the Lord Jesus Christ says: 'I am a worm. I am the tola.' He had to be crushed to death that you and I might be clothed in glory. The glorious garments of our salvation come from his shed blood, suffering and death.'[13]

In Matthew's account three groups of people mock and scoff at Jesus taunting and ridiculing him. A reminder of Isaiah 53: 3: 'He was despised and rejected by men, a man of sorrows and acquainted with grief.' While it is speculative, I believe we can imagine that on the cross Jesus would also have remembered the suffering servant described so vividly in Isaiah 53, and with which he would have indentified himself during his ministry and crucifixion. This may have helped him to make sense of what was happening on the cross as God's will.

12-13 Many bulls encompass me, strong bulls of Basham surround me: they open wide their mouths at me like a ravening and roaring lion.

Jesus was likely to be aware of the terrifying animal imagery David used to describe his enemies. These can stand for the powerful opposition of the chief priests and scribes, to Annas and Caiphas, the high priests who were responsible for his arrest and trial and Pilate who condemned him to death. The animal imagery represents a frightening picture of predatory behaviour towards Jesus. He was surrounded by a pack of vicious evildoers.

'These animal metaphors symbolise vicious threats to life. The conventional pair of the lion and bull represents the epitome of power.'[14] The lion, bull and dogs represent an image of powerful beasts ready to pounce and finish off and kill their prey.

14-18   I am poured out like water and all my bones are out of joint, my heart is like wax it is melted within my breast: my strength is dried up like a potsherd, and my tongue cleaves to my jaws: thou dost lay me in the jaws of death. Dogs are round about me: a company of evildoers encircle me: they have pierced my hands and feet, I can count all my bones - they stare and gloat over me: they divide my garments among them and for my raiment they cast lots.

Verses 14-15 portray a terrifying image of the sense of desperation of Jesus' crucifixion. His life is ebbing away. He is literally physically being torn apart on the cross. This paints a picture of extreme physical distress and emotional fragmentation and an awareness by Jesus that he is dying. 'The bones of his hands, arms, shoulders and pelvis are out of joint. Visualise the suffering this would cause. The profuse perspiration caused intense suffering: the action of the heart was affected. His strength was exhausted and extreme thirst took place. His hands and feet were pierced.'[15] These verses also describe extreme emotional, psychological and spiritual trauma as Jesus feels overwhelmed by what is happening to him. His heart like wax is melted away - is he also dying of a broken heart as his relationship with God is being ruptured and torn apart? He is becoming aware that his life is ebbing away and that God is 'laying him in the dust of death.' Jesus is as good as dead. His bodily parts are failing and he is desolate as he is aware God is allowing him to die.

This presents us with an unfathomable mystery. For while we can understand Christ died for sinners, there is an element of mystery as God whom Christ knows can save him, is not doing so. In Christ God was reconciling the world to himself - 2 Cor. 5: 19 - but on the cross God is holding back from saving Jesus. The reality is that on the cross Jesus felt as brittle as a potsherd, so brittle that he could crumble - fall apart. In reality Jesus was defenceless against the 'dogs' that surrounded him. A term used for human agents of evil. The scavengers who will benefit from his death gloated over his predicament as they cast lots for his garments - Matt. 27: 33. 'I can count all my bones' implies Jesus bones were so out of joint and protruding he was aware of his body being distorted. Jesus is overwhelmed by what is happening to him. If there was a time for Jesus' faith in God to fail him it was now. Abandoned, isolated, powerless, ridiculed, his body broken and distorted by his physical suffering and inner spiritual torment. This is holy ground to reflect on in holy adoration.

19-21   But thou O Lord be not far off! O thou my help hasten to my aid! Deliver my soul from the sword, my darling from the power of the dog! Save me from the mouth of the lion, my afflicted soul from the horns of the wild oxen. You have heard me!

Although Jesus only uttered the first and last verses of Psalm 22 on the cross he would have been familiar with all of this psalm. Aware that it contained a prayer for deliverance from death and his enemies. Aware that God had heard the psalmist. During his crucifixion we can imagine Jesus praying in his spirit for his deliverance. 'My darling' in v 20 can be translated in a number of ways. 'Solitary one' - 'dear one' - 'beloved one'[16] or 'my only-one' that emphasises his dignity and deity as the only begotten Son of God.[17] The horns of the wild ox represented the altar of sacrifice that had four horns one at each corner. On this altar animals were sacrificed. Christ was the perfect sacrifice for sins and his prayer was to be saved after he had born our sins on this altar.[18] 'You have heard me' is a cry of triumph, not despair. It marks the moment at which the period of darkness passes and Jesus having suffered a true alienation from the Father as punishment for our sins, becomes aware again of God's presence.[19]

22-31   I will tell of your name to my brethren: in the midst of the great congregation I will praise you: You who fear the Lord praise him! All you sons of Jacob glorify him, and stand in awe of him all of you sons of Israel! For he has not despised or abhorred the affliction of the afflicted: and he has not hidden his face from him, but he has heard when he cried to him. From you comes my praise in the great congregation: my vows I will pay before those who fear him. The afflicted shall eat and be satisfied: those who seek him shall praise the Lord! May your hearts live for ever! All the ends of the earth shall remember and turn to the Lord: and all the families of the nations shall worship before him. For dominion belongs to the Lord and he rules over the nations. Yes to him shall all the proud of the earth bow down: before him shall bow all who go down to the dust and he who cannot keep himself alive. Posterity shall serve him: men shall tell of the Lord to the coming generation and proclaim his deliverance to a people yet unborn that he has done this.

In these verses while David praised the Lord for his deliverance when we see them as a messianic prophecy pointing to Christ they take on a new meaning. Not only are we completely speechless at the dramatic reversal of fortune in v 22, we are equally stunned by the ecstatic nature of v 22-31 that describes it, but also points to Jesus' resurrection. These verses bear witness that Jesus was assured his Father had heard him and that his atonement was accepted and that untold generations of people in the future would be saved and become his brothers and sisters.

Hebrews 2: 11-12 sees Jesus as the one whom Psalm 22: 22 is speaking about: 'For it was fitting that he for whom and by whom all things exist, in bringing many sons to glory, should make the pioneer of their salvation perfect through suffering. For he who sanctifies and those who are sanctified have all one origin. This is why Jesus is not ashamed to call them brethren saying: 'I will proclaim your name to my brethren, in the midst of the congregation I will praise you.' In v 22-31 Jesus testifies to God's salvation to an ever widening circle of people. In v 22 it is to 'my brethren' - the Jewish nation and   this had a partial fulfillment when Jesus appeared to the disciples after his resurrection. In v 25 it is to 'the great assembly or congregation' - this is to the Early Church and includes the Gentiles. In v 27 it is to all 'the ends of the earth' and 'all the families of the nations' - that is to the Christians throughout the earth and all the nations. In v 30 it is to 'the coming generation' and in v 31 it is to 'a people yet unborn.' This final ambitious witness to a group of people highlights the universal proclamation of the truth of the Gospel down the ages. What is striking about this reference to this ever increasing circle of people is that in turn each group is exhorted to praise or worship the Lord, for the salvation he has secured through the death and resurrection of Christ.

PSALM 24

THE KING OF GLORY

B. Pickett informs us that in the history of the Church Psalm 24 was used at funeral services where Christ guides the believer from the grave to paradise. 'The Orthodox burial still retains a remnant of this bold imagery. For a priest the whole of Psalm 24 is chanted but at all funerals the body is laid to rest and the priest scatters dust upon it in the sign of the cross with the words:

The Lord's is the earth and its fullness:
the world and all who dwell therein.

The earth of the grave is claimed by its Creator and Sovereign in whose name it is to take and cherish the departed until resurrection. The dramatic dialogue of the psalm demanding that the gates of death lift up their heads for the King of glory is illustrated in ikons of the resurrection. The risen Christ descends to raise the dead from their dark captivity, shattering the doors of hell and scattering broken hinges, bolts and keys. For Christians brought up in the synagogue this psalm had an immediate resonance with the resurrection because it was the psalm set for the first day after the Sabbath, that is Easter Day... The singing of Psalm 24 at the Easter Vigil may also have inspired the composition of the canticle *'Te Deum'* (Psalm 95) with its celebration of Christ as the King of glory opening the kingdom of heaven to all believers.'[1]

The liturgical context of Psalm 24 is identified as the occasion when David brought the ark of the covenant to Jerusalem. The ark was the gold-plated chest that contained the stone tablets of the law given to Moses on Mount Sinai by the Lord and it signified his invisible presence amongst his people. The background to this is found in 1 Chron. ch. 15-16 and 2 Samuel ch. 6. However, what is surprising is that none of the liturgy of the song of celebration that marked this occasion in 1 Chron. 16 is alluded to in Psalm 24. Whereas, 1 Chron. 16: 23-34 is recorded in the whole of Psalm 96. Also, 1 Chron. 16: 8-22 is also recorded in Psalm 105: 1-15. But, one new theme that is introduced in Psalm 24 and stands out and which is not included in 1 Chron. 15-16 is that of the 'King of glory.' The importance of the occasion in Psalm 24 is captured by D. Kidner: 'That unique occasion,' its installation in Israel's royal city, was in many ways, 'the greatest day in David's life.'[2] M. Wilcox perceives there was something even more significant than the greatest day in David's life. It marked the end of a far longer journey for the ark to Jerusalem from where it had originally been constructed by Moses at Mount Sinai. 'One might even say that the day of the ark's arrival was in one sense the climax of all Bible history up to that point.'[3] But, this was not as significant as the occasions this Messianic Psalm prophetically points to - when Jesus the 'King of glory' actually entered Jerusalem on Palm Sunday and also when he ascended into heaven.

The kingship of God is a central theme in the Old Testament and can be traced to Exodus 15: 18. 'Psalm 24 is one of the central texts for understanding the breadth and the significance of this concept: the kingship of the Lord is not merely a religious affirmation - it is a basis of worship and praise. Those who worship are those who recognise the kingship, who accept the rule of the sovereign God. But the genius of the psalm lies in the linking together of the cosmological belief and historical experience…The recognition of the kingship of God must result in the worship of God by those who recognise his royal authority: to worship presupposes moral integrity - and that in a sense is the central point of the psalm.'[4]

Psalm 24 readily divides into three sections: v 1-2, 3-6 and 7-10. J. Crenshaw has an interesting stance about the second section when he speaks of the qualities required to approach *sacred space.* Whereas, in the third section it is the King of glory who is coming to enter this *sacred space.*[5] This psalm was likely to have been used in a procession with the ark with all three sections in turn being used as a liturgical refrain. When the ark entered the temple gates this was of great significance in the religious culture of the ancient world. In Mesopotamia and Canaan, the god who was victorious over the primeval sea (creation) gained kingship and the right to a temple-palace to represent his sovereignty. The entrance of the ark was the dramatic representation of the Lord's identity as sovereign of the world.[6]

1-2   The earth is the Lord's and the fullness thereof, the world and those who dwell therein: for he founded it upon the seas and established it upon the rivers.

At first glance v 1-2 appear disconnected from the rest. But, they are a declaration of God as Creator who possesses the earth and reigns over it. Crenshaw says about them: 'a resounding declaration of possession... lest anyone miss the sweeping scope of this utterance, however, the psalmist elaborates the implications of the initial claim: 'The Lord's are the earth and all that fills it, the world and its inhabitants' - v 1. In short nothing outside the world of observable phenomena lies beyond the Lord's domain.'[7] This is a indeed a universal claim of God's ownership that extends beyond the boundaries of Israel. God not only possesses all the earth and reigns as king over it - the earth rests secure because he has established it. This speaks of an 'existential reassurance' in the face of global anxieties.[8] And if the earth belongs to the Lord and he reigns over it his presence is to be found in it.

3-6   Who shall ascend the hill of the Lord? And who shall stand in his holy place? He who has clean hands and a pure heart, who does not lift up his soul to what is false, and does not swear deceitfully. He will receive blessing from the Lord and vindication from the God of his salvation. Such is the generation of those who seek him, who seek the face of the God of Jacob.

Psalm 24 gradually builds to an ecstatic climax and a crescendo of celebration and worship in the last section. The prelude to this in the second section identifies those who alongside the 'king of glory' would also ascend the hill of the Lord and stand in his holy place and presence.

As they approach in joyful expectation the people ask the questions and the priest replies - v 3-4. A similar but more extended entrance liturgy is in Psalm 15: 1-5 and the requirements are considerably more comprehensive. These are clearly detailed regulations for entering *sacred space* and in Psalm 24 we have a shortened version. This reminds us that Jesus said in Matt: 5: 8: 'Blessed are the pure in heart for they shall see God.'

M. Wilcox memorably cites the requirements of entering God's presence with clean heart and pure hands when he says:

> To meet God there required right living, right thinking, a right relationship with him and a right relationship with one's fellows. But, these things were a righteousness (vindication) which could only be received, not achieved: things which the God who saves from sin gives to *those who seek him.*[9]

These entrance liturgies acted as a means of self examination on the way to worship the Lord and enter into his presence. They enabled people to examine their hearts and minds before the euphoric celebration of the entrance of the King took place - v 7-10. A timely reminder for Christians to do the same. Also a timely reminder of Micah 6: 8: 'He has showed you, O man, what is good: and what does the Lord require of you, but to do justice, to love mercy and to walk humbly with your God?'

7-10   Lift up your heads, O gates! and be lifted up, O ancient doors! that the King of glory may come in. Who is the King of glory? The Lord, strong and mighty, the Lord mighty in battle! Lift up your heads, O gates! and be lifted up, O ancient doors! that the King of glory may come in. Who is this King of glory? The Lord of hosts, he is the King of glory!

The ecstatic, joyful celebratory climax in v 7-10 comes alive when we imagine an antiphonal liturgical refrain involving a chorus-choir who sing: 'Lift up your heads, O gates! and be lifted up O ancient doors! that the King of glory may come in' - followed by a voice within the Temple walls saying: 'Who is this King of glory.' A spokesman, perhaps a priest for the king replies: 'The Lord strong and mighty.' The chorus-choir respond again: 'Lift up your heads, O you gates' - followed by the spokesman, perhaps a priest saying: 'Who is he, this King of glory?' Then everyone joins in with the refrain: 'The Lord of Hosts - he is the King of glory.'[10]

The implication of v 3-6 is that the Lord was on Mount Zion and the people were seeking to come into *sacred space* into his presence. However, in v 7-10 the scene changes as the King of glory seeks entrance into his sanctuary on the hill of the Lord! The title 'the King of glory' occurs five times in these verses and is unique in that it is found nowhere else in Scripture. (We have the God of glory in Acts 7: 2: 'the Lord of glory' in 1 Cor. 2: 8: and 'the Father of glory' in Eph. 1: 17). But, only in Psalm 24 do we have 'the King of glory.'[11] J. M. Boice poignantly points out that Psalm 24 was always used in worship on the first day of the week. Therefore, we may assume that these were the words being recited by the temple priests on Palm Sunday when Christ mounted a donkey and ascended the approach to Jerusalem. The people who went along with him exclaimed: 'Hosanna to the Son of David! Blessed is he who comes in the name of the Lord! Hosanna in the highest!' - Matt. 21: 9. Whereas, inside the Temple the priests were reciting Psalm 24: 9-10: 'Lift up your heads, O gates: and be lifted up, O ancient doors! that the King of glory may come in. Who is this King of glory? The Lord of hosts, he is the King of glory!'[12]

The entrance liturgy in v 7-10 is repeated to ascertain and confirm that the King of glory is the victorious warrior, the Lord of hosts. It is of interest to note that Psalm 29 describes the Lord who manifests his glory over nature and sits enthroned for ever as King. In a liturgical refrain, the heavenly host ascribe to the Lord glory and strength and worship that is due to his name - v 1-2. The link with Psalm 24 when the Lord arrives to enter through the doors of the temple on Zion is a recognition of his glory as King. But, the King of glory is also identified as the Lord of hosts. 'It is the title the Lord bears as royal resident in Zion (Psalm 84: 1, 3) whose power makes the city invulnerable. The title refers to the hosts who surround the Lord's heavenly throne and who praise and consult him and carry out his decisions as sovereign of the world. In Psalm 89: 5-14 there is a long description of the Lord of hosts in which all the theological features of Psalm 24 appear. It is especially important for verses 3-6 that righteousness, justice, steadfast love and faithfulness are said to be features of the reign of the Lord of hosts. This explains the necessity of the character of the righteous for those who go to stand in his royal presence.'[13]

In modern lectionaries Psalm 24 is used on Palm Sunday on Jesus' entry into Jerusalem. It has also had a long association with the celebration of the ascension of Jesus on Ascension Day. In this context Jesus is portrayed as the Messianic King who has gained victory over death and sin: and who has entered the heavenly city of Jerusalem to reign at the right hand of God as the King of Glory. The Suffering Servant and Saviour on the cross is the victorious warrior who enters into his eternal glory. We read in Revelation 14: 1: 'Then I looked and lo, on Mount Zion stood the Lamb' - this gives us a vision of the ascended Christ the King of glory. The book of Revelation also gives us a prophetic vision of the new heavenly Jerusalem: 'Then I saw a new heaven and a new earth: for the first heaven and the first earth had passed away, and the sea was no more. And I saw the holy city, new Jerusalem, coming down out of heaven from God' - 20: 1-2.

PSALM 40

THE INCARNATION

Psalm 40 contains some very striking theological features. Psalm 70 is a repeat of Psalm 40: 13-17 and there is an unorthodox start to Psalm 40 as v. 1-11 are a complex song of praise for deliverance followed by a prayer for help. This is unusual as prayer for help almost always precedes praise. Some of the contents of the Messianic Psalms clearly refer to the psalmist while other parts refer to Christ. This is certainly true of Psalm 40 as Hebrews 10: 5-7 refers to Psalm 40: 6-8 and act as a commentary on it. This points to the incarnation of Christ who fulfilled v 6-8. But, in v. 1-5 David testifies to God's deliverance while he patiently waited for it. M. Wilcox says, 'The old Latin title of Psalm 40, *Expectans, expectavi,* indicates both its eagerness and the Hebrew that lies behind the words *waited patiently,* namely a doubling of the verb: 'Expectantly I expected the Lord to act.'[1] David's patient waiting for deliverance from the desolate pit and miry bog are metaphors to describe his experience and are not to be taken literally. But, like a number of Biblical commentators we can see a link with Jeremiah 38: 1-13, who found himself in a cistern - a pit full of mud from which he was rescued.

6-8   Sacrifice and offering you do not desire: but you have given me an open ear. Burnt offerings and sin offering you have not required. Then I said, 'Lo I come: in the roll of the book it is written of me, I delight to do your will O my God: your law is written within my heart.

1 Sam. 13: 8-14 records the first time Saul was disobedient to the Lord that resulted in his rejection as king. Psalm 40: 6 is a quote from 1 Sam. 15. 22. This is the Old

Testament background to this verse where Saul the first king of Israel after a victory over the Amalekites offered a sacrifice to God. But, the Lord rejected this because he was not completely obedient to what the Lord specifically commanded him. As a result of this second incidence of disobedience Samuel tells Saul once again that the Lord has rejected him as king. Saul immediately acknowledges his sin to Samuel and asks for forgiveness and an opportunity to worship the Lord. It is surprising that Psalm 40: 6 does not quote more fully 1 Sam. 15: 22 - where obedience to the voice of the Lord is preferred as opposed to sacrifices: 'Behold to obey is better than sacrifice and to hearken than the fat of rams.'

In its original context v 6-8 are David's response to God's deliverance and this involves the ritual offering of thanksgiving and praise. In v 7 he reaffirms his commitment to do God's will because his law is within his heart. This is accompanied by his testimony in the great congregation. In effect this is a commentary on v 4: 'Blessed is the man who makes the Lord his trust' - the man in this instance is David who affirms his love and obedience to the Lord. This is in contrast to Saul who was disobedient. (Although later in his life David's sin with Bathsheba brought severe judgement and tragedy to his family).

> What is inscribed with an indelible ink on the heart is equivalent to the personal disposition: rather than external obligation this is a desire that springs from within. The voluntary sacrifice of the will to God is the most costly and the most desired offering.[2]

There are different ways of translating v 6b 'you have given me an open ear.' The Hebrew word for opened is *karah* and this can also be 'but my ears you have pierced.' This refers to the Hebrew servant in Exodus 21: 1-6 and Deut. 15: 12-18. A man became a slave because of debt or bankruptcy and he sold himself as a slave for 6 years or until the year of the jubilee, when on both occasions he could be set free. But, after 6 years a slave could legally be taken to the judges and declare his commitment to stay permanently with his master rather than go free. The 6 years were compulsory but after that it was love for his master that relinquished his right to freedom. When this occurred as a sign of his permanent commitment his master placed his ear next to the door post and made a small hole with an awl.[3]

We read in Hebrews 10: 5-7, consequently when Christ came into the world he said:

> "Sacrifices and offerings you have not desired, but a body you have prepared for me: in burnt offerings and sin offerings you have taken no pleasure. Then I said, 'Lo I have come to do your will, O God' as it is written of me in the roll of the book."

Psalm 40: 6-8 and Heb. 10: 5-7 both proclaim the mystery of the incarnation of the Messiah. Biblical commentators suggest that 'my ear you have pierced' becomes 'a body you have prepared for me.' Here, the author of Hebrews quotes the Septuagint version of the psalm. The Greek version of the Old Testament translated in Alexandria in the 3rd century. The link between ear and body represents obedience to God by Christ and a sign of love in his incarnation. 'Lo I come to do your will' is a unique insight into a conversation between Christ and the Father. This represents Christ's perfect obedience that embraced both his divinity and humanity in his incarnation. We glimpse two examples of Christ obedience in the Gospels that are supreme examples of doing God's will. The first involves his temptations in the wilderness by the devil where on three occasions Jesus chose to be obedient to God - Matt. 4: 1-11. The second is found in Jesus' prayer in the Garden of Gethsemane when he submitted to the Father's will to go to the cross - Matt. 26: 36-39.

'I delight to do your will - your law is within my heart' eloquently speaks of Christ's sinlessness. This enabled him as our great high priest to be the perfect sacrifice for sin. One aspect of the incarnation from Psalm 40 which the Book of Hebrews highlights is the permanent nature of the sacrifice of Christ that made obsolete the perpetual sacrifices of the Old Testament. 'It is this theme of sacrifice which made Psalm 40 an appropriate passage for use as one of the proper psalms on Good Friday during the development of Christian worship.'[4] 'Verses 6-8 have always had special importance in the use of the psalm in liturgy and theology because the letter to the Hebrews uses these verses as the words of Christ and gives a new answer to the question of who speaks.'[5]

9-10   I have told the glad news of deliverance in the great congregation: lo, I have not restrained my lips as you know O Lord. I have not hidden your saving help within my heart. I have spoken of your faithfulness and your salvation: I have not concealed your steadfast love and your faithfullness from the great congregation.

Throughout The Psalter you get the impression there is an obligation to testify to God's goodness and salvation. Verse 3 implies that it is the Lord himself who is the source of the inspiration for praise to be offered to him. Moreover, that this has an evangelistic impact on those who listen to it. Spurgeon mentions in Christ's ministry he taught openly in the temple and was not ashamed to be a faithful witness. What was in our master's heart he poured forth in holy eloquence from his lips.[6]

PSALM 45

THE BRIDEGROOM

Psalm 45 is unique in that it is like no other psalm in The Psalter. Its focus is not primarily on the Lord but the bridegroom and bride. Such is the difference that it would clearly not be out of place in the Song of Songs. This Royal Psalm about a royal wedding is like an ecstatic sonorous love song, with evocative metaphors describing a magnificent and splendid occasion. But, as we shall see, there is a Messianic interpretation to it, as the marriage can be seen as an allegory of Christ and the Church and the heavenly wedding of the Christ the Bridegroom to the Church the Bride.

The title to Psalm 45 is: 'To the choirmaster: according to the Lilies. A Maskil of the Sons of Korah: a love song.' Maskil means teaching or instruction and there are four psalms that have the title 'Lilies.' They are for the springtime and Passover season. Concerning the theme 'a love song,' the Hebrew is plural and is *'loveliness' or 'beloved ones'* It is the word rendered amiable in Psalm 84: 1. It is used especially of those who are loved by God - Deut: 33: 12. It can also be interpreted as a 'song of the beloved.'[1] One notable feature of Psalm 45:1 is that the author identifies himself as a professional writer not unlike a court poet. This is a unique introduction in The Psalter and the language is so unusual it borders on the ecstatic. H. Gunkel translates v 1 as: 'My heart overflows with inspired words.'[2] Although there is not a definite conclusion Biblical commentators speculate as to which royal wedding Psalm 45 refers to. It has been suggested it is the marriage of Solomon to the princess of Egypt or to a princess of Tyre. Yet, because the language of Psalm 45 is so splendid its interpretation points to a Jewish King who is much more exalted than Solomon. A. Maclaren says: 'Either we have here a piece of poetical exaggeration far beyond the limits of poetic license, or 'a greater than Solomon is here.'[3]

It is of interest to note the cultural background of such a wedding as the context for its interpretation. On the wedding day the attendants and friends of both the bride and groom arrived at their respective homes to help them dress for the occasion. When the bridegroom was ready he went with his attendants in a grand procession through the city streets to fetch the bride. This was followed by a second procession of the entire wedding party, both the bride and groom's entourage, from the bride's home back to the bridegroom's. And at his home there would be a wedding feast that could last as long as a week or two.[4]

1-9   My heart overflows with a godly theme: I address my verses to the king: my tongue is like the pen of a ready scribe. You are the fairest of the sons of men: grace is poured forth upon your lips: therefore God has blessed you for ever. Gird your sword upon your thigh, O mighty one, in your glory and majesty! In your majesty ride forth victoriously for the cause of truth and to defend the right: let your right hand teach your dread deeds! Your arrows are sharp in the heart of the king's enemies: the peoples fall under you. Your divine throne endures for ever and ever. Your royal scepter is a scepter of equity, you love righteousness and hate wickedness. Therefore, God, your God, has anointed you with the oil of gladness above your fellows: your robes are all fragrant with myrrh and aloes and cassia. From ivory palaces stringed instruments make you glad: daughters are among your ladies of honour: at your right hand stands the queen in gold of Ophir.

Psalm 45:1 is the introduction and v 16-17 the conclusion penned by the poet. In v. 2-9 he addresses the bridegroom and in v 10-15 the bride. In the former verses the poet lavishly extols, flatters and praises the glory, virtues and victories of the groom as king. He eulogises about his aesthetic glory - v 2, the glory of his speech - v 2, his kingly glory - v 6-7 and his divine, royal glory - v 8-9. Yet, no king in Israel's history could claim to have fulfilled this idealistic portrait of kingship - not even David or Solomon. These verses highlight the king is a mighty warrior who defends the cause of truth and right and defeats his enemies - v 3-5. In his reign, throne and sceptre are dedicated to the support of righteousness and opposition to wickedness so that his elevation by God to be the anointed is justified - v 6-7.[5] T. Wilson attributes these qualities to Christ when he says: 'We see the excellency of His Person, the equity of His rule, the eternity of His throne and the ecstasy of His heart.'[6] In hindsight we can see that Christ fulfilled the inspired aspirations that pointed to the Messianic King in Psalm 45. Only he was a spiritual warrior defeating sin, death and Satan.

The author first highlights the king's beautiful appearance and gracious speech. But, these attributes are identified as a gift of God's divine and eternal blessing. When we consider the term 'fairest' applied to Christ we focus on his ascended glory. But we know from Isaiah 53: 2-3 that during our Lord's life his appearance was considered undistinguished and he was despised. Now in the Book of Revelation we have heavenly descriptions of Christ (ch. 1: 12-16, 5: 6-10, 19: 11-16). When we consider the phrase: 'grace is poured forth upon your lips' - (grace occurs in only two psalms 45 and 84) - P. C. Craigie says: 'It is the king's royal attributes and divinely approved functions which give rise to such celebration. Thus the first objects of beauty are the king's 'lips,' not because of their physical appearance, but because they are anointed with 'grace.' Thus anointed they speak words of grace and kindness to the royal subjects and the gracious speech in turn evokes the divine blessing of the king.'[7] The king's speech is deemed to be gracious and presumably his words reflect his rule of righteousness, justice and truth, qualities mentioned in v 4, 6-7. Presumably, they also reflect his character. Christ the Messiah anointed with and full of the Holy Spirit, displayed these gracious qualities in his teaching, his encounters with individuals and in his ministry.

The inspired claim of Psalm 45: 6-8 is quoted in Hebrews 1: 8-9 about Christ: 'But of the Son God says: 'Your throne, O God, endures for ever and ever. The righteous sceptre is the sceptre of your kingdom. You have loved righteousness and hated lawlessness: therefore God, your God has anointed you, with the oil of gladness above your brethren.' The astonishing claim and truth of v 8 is that God's Son, Christ, the Messiah is God and he has a throne and it is eternal. At oriental feasts oil was poured on the heads of distinguished guests and the anointing with oil of the king was a sign of being chosen by God as in the case of David - I Sam. 16: 13 for his royal task. In the context of the wedding ceremony the king is anointed with oil as part of the joyful celebrations. 'The Hebrew word behind *anointed* v 7 is from the same root as *messiah.*'[8] Although no Biblical commentator makes much of it and its importance is overlooked the king has been anointed by God with 'the oil of gladness above his companions.' Apart from the joy connected to the king's royal wedding, the oil of gladness is specifically given to him a result of his love for righteousness and truth. These words are applied to Christ in Heb. 1: 8 and indicate his abundant, overflowing joy in his love for righteousness and truth. Christ is 'rewarded with superior joy.'[9]

In Heb. 12: 2 we read, 'Jesus the pioneer and perfecter of our faith who for the joy that was set before him endured the cross, despising the shame and is seated at the right hand of the throne of God.' We can glimpse aspects of Jesus' joy in the gospels from the healings and miracles he performed and from the individuals he met. He would have been joyful at seeing the kingdom of God having an impact in peoples' lives and when people responded to his teaching about God as Father. Jesus' joy is also seen in John 15: 1: 'These things I have spoken to you, that my joy may be in you and that your joy may be full.' F. F. Bruce says: 'It is not difficult to trace an affinity between the joy of which our author speaks here and the joy to which Jesus himself makes repeated reference in the upper room discourses of the Fourth Gospel. He tells his disciples there of his desire that his joy may be in them, so that their joy may be full (John 15: 11: cf. 16: 20-24): and in his high priestly prayer he asks the Father 'that they may have my joy fulfilled in themselves.' So here the 'joy set before him' is not something for himself alone, but something to be shared with those for whom he died as sacrifice and lives as high priest.'[10]

Psalm 45: 8-9 introduce a change of scene. Up to this point the king has been described as a victorious warrior upholding righteousness and truth. Now he is beautifully dressed as a bridegroom who will meet his bride in a ceremony full of gladness, rejoicing and happiness. In the New Testament marriage is an allegory for Christ as the Bridegroom and the Church as his Bride - Matt. 9: 15, John 3: 29 and Eph. 5: 22-23. Revelation 19: 7-9 says: 'Hallelujah! For the Lord our God the Almighty reigns. Let us rejoice and exult and give him the glory, *for the marriage of the Lamb has come and his Bride has made herself ready:* it was granted her to be clothed with fine linen, bright and pure.' J. L. Mays says, 'Christians have traditionally understood Psalm 45 as a song of love between Christ and his Church.'[11] The idea of a marriage between Christ and the Church is not such a revolutionary idea when we consider the Old Testament prophets who likened God's relationship with Israel as a marriage. We see this in Hosea 1-3, Jeremiah 2 Ezekiel 16 and Isaiah 62: 5.

Psalm 45: 8-9 mention the bridegroom's wedding clothes being fragrant with myrrh, aloes and cassia. After his anointing the groom would be dressed in royal robes tinged with the fragrance of these precious spices. Myrrh would be used in the anointing oil and it is also found in the perfumes lovers would romantically use as in the Song of Solomon 4: 14. The beautiful aroma of perfumed spices adds an element of romance to the royal occasion. This reminds us of being clothed with the fragrance of Christ - the lovely qualities of his personality. The Apostle Paul touches on this in 2 Cor. 2: 14-15 where he contrasts the impact of his ministry with that of the false apostles. 'But thanks be to God who in Christ always leads us in triumphal procession, and through us spreads the fragrance of the knowledge of him everywhere. For we are the aroma of Christ to God among those who are being saved.' The use of the metaphor 'the fragrance of the knowledge of Christ' is a striking image that describes the ministry of Paul. In contrast although the false apostles in Corinth preached about Christ they were really only commending themselves. But, Paul does nothing of the sort. He knows appearances can be deceptive and ministry can be egocentric when it is not flowing from a deep commitment to exalt Christ. The fragrance of Christ is an evocative metaphor and it is an integral aspect of Paul's philosophy of ministry. It entails our love and friendship being infused with the attractive aroma of the personality of Christ.

The mention in v 8-9 of ivory palaces describes an opulent and sumptuous residence the like of which King Ahab built - 1 Kings 22: 39. But, these palaces are not constructed from ivory but would have been decorated with ivory and on this royal occasion stringed instruments played. The ivory palace speaks of the glory that Christ in his incarnation left behind in the heavenly places when he was born in Bethlehem. There is a hymn by Henry Barraclough, 'Out of the Ivory Palaces.' Below is the 1st verse and chorus.

> My Lord has garments so wondrous fine
> And myrrh their texture fills:
> Its fragrance reached to this heart of mine
> With joy my being thrills.

Chorus
Out of the ivory palaces
Into a world of woe:
Only his great eternal love
Made my Saviour go.

10-15   Hear, O daughter, consider and incline you ear:
forget your people and your father's house: and
the king will desire your beauty. Since he is your
Lord bow to him: the people of Tyre will court
your favour with gifts, the richest of the people
with all kinds of wealth. The princess is decked
in her chamber with gold-woven robes: in many
coloured robes she is led to the king, with her
virgin companions, her escort in her train. With
joy and gladness they are led along as they enter
the palace of the king.

In v 10-15 the poet introduces a change of scene extolling
the bride. The focus is now on the royal bride, the
queen and her beauty. The Hebrew for queen is *shegal* not
the usual *malkah* or *gebireh. Shegal* is a rare and unusual
designation of a consort used of Chaldeans or Persian
queens that indicates the queen-consort here is a
Gentile.[12] In v 10-12 despite the joyful anticipation of her
wedding day the royal bride may have felt anxious
and overwhelmed by the occasion. Although it is a
momentous occasion for her she is leaving the comfort
and security of her father's home and people. With an
engaging and tender touch the poet reassures the bride
that her future is assured as the king will desire her
beauty. An expression of his love for her and a sign that
his royal bride will be held in esteem. Verses 13-15
succinctly describe the beautiful wedding dress of the
princess, along with the procession of the royal bride with
her virgin companions. They are full of joy and gladness
as they enter the king's palace for the wedding ceremony.
The finest wedding robes and the beauty of the bride

who is ready to meet her husband reminds us of Christ
adorning the Church with holy garments in Eph. 5: 25-28:

> Christ loved the Church and gave himself up for
> her, that he might sanctify her, having cleansed
> her by the washing of water with the word, that he
> might present the Church to himself in splendour,
> without spot or wrinkle or any such thing, that she
> might be holy and without blemish.

16-17   Instead of your fathers shall be your sons: you will
        make them princes in all the earth. I will cause
        your name to be celebrated in all generations:
        therefore the peoples will praise you for ever and
        ever.

One cannot help but feel a sense of disappointment as the
poet fails to describe the royal wedding. It is left to the
imagination to picture the bride and groom making their
vows to one another and to visualise the interior of the
king's palace and the important guests who attended and
the expensive gifts they gave to the royal couple. The poet
ends Psalm 45 with a blessing addressed specifically to
the bridegroom and one may assume v 13-15 are also for
his benefit. The significance of having sons is clearly
to maintain the continuity of the royal dynasty and
to perpetuate the king's name. The poet possibly saw this
being more important than a description of the wedding
ceremony. Through human love in Psalm 45 we can see
an allegory of Christ and the Church. P. C. Craigie
says: 'For Psalm 45, in its second meaning develops
not only the allegory of love, but also that of royalty.
Christ, the King, has been enthroned by God and rules in
righteousness. The Church, the Bride, is called upon to
leave home and worship the King. But, the ultimate
blessing of the marriage is that of children, the future
generations through whom the kingdom would flourish.'[13]

Psalm 45 ends with a benediction specifically connected to the name of the king so that his name is immortalised for ever. We can trace this to David and the covenant the Lord made with him that one of his descendents would always be on the throne. We can also apply this to the name of Christ who was descended from David. 'Therefore, God has highly exalted him and bestowed on him the Name which is above every name, that at the Name of Jesus every knee should bow, in heaven and on earth' - Phil. 2: 9-10. The hymn by Frederick Woodfield written in 1855 extols the name of Jesus. The following are 2 verses and the chorus.

There is a Name I love to hear
I love to speak its worth.
It sounds like music in my ear
The sweetest Name on earth.

Chorus
O how I love Jesus
O how I love Jesus
O how I love Jesus
Because He first loved me!

Jesus the Name I love so well
The Name I love to hear.
No saint on earth its worth can tell
No heart conceive how dear.

PSALM 68

THE ASCENSION

Biblical commentators point out Psalm 68 is complex and almost legendary in posing difficulties in interpretation. This is partly due to a number of disconnected elements - themes and a corrupted text that is likely to have been revised by a liturgical redactor in a cultic context. It contains an ancient allusion to Numbers 10: 35 along with a number of other ancient images and phenomena. The style includes speech and narrative, description, prayer and praise, historical interpretation and eschatological nuances.[1] Despite the apparent difficulties in understanding this psalm, as we shall see, it is a coherent unit with diverse elements.

The beginning of Psalm 68 speaks of the appearance of God in the midst of his people and does so in the form of the ancient cultic liturgy. It is a celebratory psalm of liturgical jubilation and ecstatic exaltation of God's salvation for the righteous, the underprivileged and weak, as opposed to the rebellious and wicked. There is the joyful celebration of the reign and victory of God the divine warrior over his enemies. 'Whatever its uncertainties, to read it or hear it read is to experience something of the awesome, wonderful majesty of the warrior God who saves his people and brings in his kingdom.'[2] The cultic procession in v 26-28 suggests the use of Psalm 68 in a festival. Yet this psalm does not merely hint at a local congregational celebration by God's people. It is that. But, it is more. There is also a visionary element that can see other kings and nations coming to worship the Lord too. This is one of the prophetic truths of The Psalms in the context of worship that exhorts us to pray for our nation and the European community for this vision to be fulfilled, even in the 21st century. This is a timely reminder not to have a too narrow or too subjective outlook in our worship. One other aspect of Psalm 68 is that it can be seen as The Psalm of The Ascension of Christ from v 18.

One distinct feature of Psalm 68 is its generous allusion to the names and descriptions of God: Yahweh, Yah, Elohim, Adonai El and Shaddai: father of the fatherless and defender of widows - v 5, God our Saviour - v 19, the Sovereign Lord - v 20, my God and king - v 24, thunders with a mighty voice - v 33. There are ten stanzas in the psalm. Each highlights a different aspect of God and their scope encompasses God's mighty acts from the past to the present including a reference to the future.[3] This indicates the psalm focuses on God and his great acts of powerful deliverance and salvation that highlights the 'presence of God.' In the first half of the psalm the focus on God in v 2-17, is an emphasis on God 'arising' and his ability to scatter his enemies. This is seen by God's victorious activity in cosmic and historical matters. There is also a transition in v 16-19 as the emphasis falls upon God's choice of a dwelling place and his abiding there always. This introduces a shift to 'Yahweh will dwell there forever.' Moreover, the first part of Psalm 68 highlights the divine presence in the form of 'the coming God' who arises and comes unexpectedly and irresistibly as the victor. Whereas, in the second half of the psalm the attention is mainly directed towards God's action in relationship to his dwelling place and he is now seen as 'the abiding God.'[4]

In Psalm 68 we can discern a prologue in v 1-6 and an epilogue in v 32-35. These encompass two main sections - v 7-20 and 21-31 and contain a song about God's mighty acts and celebrate God's victorious march from Egypt to Jerusalem. Also, this is seen in the ascendency of his people and in the worshippers and vassal kingdoms that come to his footstool - v 9-13. At the same time, 'If there is a specific event for which the psalm was written and to which it refers, it is probably the occasion of the entrance of the ark into Jerusalem in the time of David recorded in 2 Samuel 6.'[5] Verses 2-11 can also be seen to highlight the ideal kingship of God, v 12-24 focus on God as the cosmic king, while v 25-36 emphasise the universal kingship of God. These divisions can be seen to be arranged around three different mountains - Sinai, Bashan and God's new abode, Zion.[6]

1-10   Let God arise and let his enemies be scattered: and
let those who hate him flee before him! As smoke
is driven away so drive them away: as wax melts
before fire, let the wicked perish before God! But
let the righteous be joyful: let them exalt before
God: let them be jubilant with joy! Sing to God,
sing praises to his name: lift up a song to him who
rides through the clouds *(or cast up a highway for
him who rides through the deserts)*: his name is
the Lord exult before him. Father of the fatherless
and protector of widows is God in his holy
habitation. God gives the desolate a home to dwell
in: he leads out the prisoners in prosperity: but the
rebellious dwell in a parched land. O God when
you went forth before your people, when you
marched through the wilderness, the earth quaked,
the heavens poured down rain at the presence
of God: Sinai quaked at the presence of God, the
God of Israel. Rain in abundance O God you did
shed abroad: you did restore your heritage as it
languished: your flock found a dwelling in it: in
your goodness O God, you did provide for the
needy.

The start of the prologue in Psalm 68: 1 invokes God to
arise and scatter his enemies and to let those who hate
him flee before him. This is a direct quote from Numbers
10: 35 that was spoken out aloud whenever the people in
the wilderness moved on at the command of the Lord.
This was also associated with the moving of the Ark. This
imagery may have acted in a liturgical sense as a reminder
of the presence of God with them. It also declares God as
the divine warrior who is victorious over his enemies and
brings salvation to his people. 'The images of the swift
disappearance of the wicked are remarkable - smoke that
is driven away and wax that melts.'[7] The invocation
in v 1-3 implies God's enemies will be defeated with
remarkable ease. They will flee and they will be driven
away: they will melt/disperse and they will perish. E.

Gerstenberger suggests these enemies are rebellious sons
or leaders from within the religious community and as
such appear in the prophetic writings (Isaiah 1: 23, 30: 1,
65: 2).[8]

Integral to the prologue is a command to God's people
to be joyful and jubilant and exalt God in praise and
worship. It is a call to join in an ecstatic celebration of
God's salvation. One of the most marvellous and sublime
truths about God's people worshipping him in the Old and
New Testaments is that it is a sharing in the joyful and
jubilant celebration of God over evil and the wicked.
The focus of the jubilant joy in v 3-4 is the Lord and his
name and this encompasses all the goodness of God's
character and salvation. In the act of worshipping the
Lord he strengthens his people and fills them with
abundant joy. In v 4 the ancient imagery of the Lord
'riding upon the clouds' is linked to the tradition of the
theophany where God comes to dwell and be present in
the sanctuary enthroned upon the wings of the cherubim
of the sacred Ark.[9] But, God is not only a divine warrior
his salvation also extends (v 5-6) to the fatherless, the
widow and the homeless. His provision for his people
is also remembered in v 7-10 when they were in the
wilderness along with the victory over his peoples'
enemies in v 11-14. 'God is praised for parenting orphans
and protecting widows. Motifs of the Exodus, the
conquest, Jerusalem, the land's fertility and vanquishing
enemies are developed in the Sinai to Zion section (v
7-18) which is an impressionistic portrayal of the Exodus
to the dwelling of God on Mount Zion.'[10]

15-20   O mighty mountain of Bashan: O many-peaked
        mountain, mountain of Bashan! Why look you
        with envy O many-peaked mountain, at the
        mount which God desired for his abode, where the
        Lord will dwell for ever? With mighty chariots,
        twice ten thousand, thousands upon thousands,

the Lord came to Sinai into the holy place. You
ascended the high mount leading captives in
your train, and receiving gifts among men, even
amongst the rebellious that the Lord may dwell
there. Blessed be the Lord who daily bears up
us: God is our salvation. Our God is a God of
salvation and to God the Lord belongs the escape
from death.

The beginning of Psalm 68 alludes to the presence of God
with his people associated with the ark of the covenant in
Numbers 10: 35: 'And whenever the ark set out Moses
said, 'Arise O Lord and let your enemies be scattered and
let them that hate you flee before you.' As the psalm
progresses the presence of God abiding with his people
is now associated with Mount Zion in Jerusalem, the
place where David chose for the ark to rest. Compared
with the majestic rugged mountains of Bashan (9000 feet
above sea level), Zion is unimpressive as it rises to
only a few hundred feet above the surrounding valleys.
Metaphorically speaking Zion should stand in awe of
Bashan. What then is the significance of the emphasis on
the mountain of Bashan being envious of Mount Zion?
J. Goldingay captures the essence of the comparison:
'Mount Hermon would regard it (Zion) as particularly
pathetic. In the immediate context so would Sinai
(associated with God's presence)...whichever mountain
Bashan eyes in resentful astonishment it does itself as a
mountain that is in its way as mighty and majestic as God.
Surely it would therefore be the mountain where God
chose to dwell!'[11] The significance of Bashan in contrast
to Zion seems somewhat enigmatic. But, presumably,
there is some significance attached to it. The choice of
Zion the smallest mountain for God to dwell on and to
manifest his presence, accompanied by the entourage of
the heavenly host of chariots, warriors and captives from
whom he received gifts may point to how impressive
God's presence and power were. It may also symbolise
the elevation of Christ as Lord who in weakness died on

the cross but who was raised in glory - as the God of our salvation not just as a warrior.

W. Wilson says, 'Psalm 68 has its historical roots in the Old Testament and the doctrinal fruits in the New Testament. The Messianic reference in v 18 is in dead centre. The background seems to be four great victory marches, three historical and one prophetic...The final victory and establishment of the kingdom...v 29-35.'[12] In Ephesians 3: 8 Paul refers to Psalm 68: 'When Christ had ascended on high he led a host of captives, and he gave gifts to men.' This refers to the ascension of Christ after his resurrection. It is possible to interpret the activity of God in Psalm 68 from the Old Testament and apply it in a messianic way to Christ. So that Christ is the one who led Israel out of Egypt through the wilderness and Christ is the one whose enemies were scattered. Christ is the one who cares for the orphan, widow and homeless and Christ is the one who received gifts from men.[13]

One difficulty presents itself when Psalm 68: 18 says, 'you received gifts from men' and Paul in Eph. 4: 8 says 'you gave gifts to men.' The major difficulty is that both the Hebrew and the Greek read 'you received gifts.' O'Brien points out that the Syriac Peshitta rendering of Psalm 68: 18 is, *'you have given gifts'* and represents a different textual tradition. The Aramaic Targum remarkably also reads, *'you gave'* rather than *'you received.'*[14] We may possibly see a comparison with Moses ascending Mount Zion and receiving the Law to give to God's people and Christ ascension where he gives gifts to them. The gifts of his grace were that some should be 'apostles, some prophets, some evangelists, some pastors and teachers' - Eph. 4: 11. It is of interest to note that the synagogues associated Psalm 68 with Pentecost that commemorated the giving of the Law to Moses on Mount Zion.[15] In contrast at Pentecost Christ gave the Holy Spirit to God's people.

Psalm 68: 18 refers to the ascent of the Lord possibly in the person of the triumphant king on Mount Zion or his presence in the ark. 'Paul applies this picture to Christ's ascension not because there was some vague analogy between the two events, but because he saw in Jesus' exaltation a further fulfilment of this triumph of God... an event of momentous theological significance as Eph. 1: 19-22 makes plain.'[16] This passage speaks of Christ's resurrection, ascension, exaltation as Lord and being seated at God's right hand as the head of the church. We can discern from the text in Eph. 1: 21-22 that Christ in his ascension has been exalted as Lord: 'far above all rule and authority and power and dominion...and he has put all things under his feet.' One of the dominant themes in Psalm 68 is the emphasis on the reign of God as king, his salvation and victory over his enemies and his triumphant ascent on Mount Zion. As we have already seen v 2-11 highlight the ideal kingship of God, v 12-24 focus on God as the cosmic king, while v 25-36 emphasise the universal kingship of God. From this perspective Christ in his ascension in like manner is also the victorious king who has brought salvation to his people and in his ascension returns triumphant over his captives-enemies. 'This establishes Christ's supremacy over the powers of evil and underlines his cosmic supremacy.'[17]

28-36   Summon your might O God: show your strength O God you who have acted for us. Because of your temple at Jerusalem kings bear gifts to you. Rebuke the beasts that dwell among the reeds, the herds of bulls with the calves of the peoples. Trample under foot those who lust after tribute: scatter the peoples who delight in war. Let bronze be brought from Egypt: let Ethiopia hasten to stretch out her hands to God. Sing to God O kingdoms of the earth: sing praises to the Lord to him who rides in the heavens, the ancient heavens: lo he sends forth his voice, his mighty voice.

Ascribe power to God whose majesty is over Israel and his power is in the skies. Terrible is God in his sanctuary, the God of Israel: he gives power and strength to his people. Blessed be God.

Psalm 68 alludes to three historical victories. The 1st is the one against the Egyptians in v 7-8. The 2nd is over the Canaanites v 9-19 (Judges 4-5). The 3rd is David's victory over the Jebusites and Philistines in v 20-28. These verses describe the song and the climax as the procession of the ark born by the priests ascend the hill and place the ark in the tent that David pitched for it on Mount Zion - (2 Sam. 6: 1, 1 Chron. 15-16). One Biblical commentator believes these three victories in Psalm 68 point to a final victory in v 29-35 at Armageddon: and the establishment of the kingdom with its earthly centre at Jerusalem.[18] O. E. Phillips sees v 24-35 describing the glorious kingdom of The Messiah ruling over the saved remnant of Israel. With v 29 referring to a new temple the Messiah will erect by his miraculous power and which the prophet Ezekiel described in ch. 40-48. He also alludes to Zechariah ch. 14 with the Messiah being King over all the earth. Zech. 14: 4-9:

> On that day the Lord's feet shall stand upon the Mount of Olives which lies before Jerusalem on the east: and the Mount of Olives shall be split in two from east to west by a very wide valley...Then the Lord your God will come and all the holy ones with him. On that day there shall be neither cold nor frost. And there shall be continuous day. On that day living waters shall flow out of Jerusalem...and the Lord will become king over all the earth: on that day the Lord will be one and his name one.[19]

J. M. Boice suggests that Psalm 68: 21-23 can point to The Messianic Age marked by the rejoicing of the righteous at the fall of Babylon described in Revelation ch. 18-19. He also suggests in v 28-35 all the nations of the world will come to worship God at Jerusalem on Mount Zion. He sees this as a 'right kind of biblical universalism.' And that the gathering of pagan nations to worship God in Jerusalem is an important theme in the prophets, particularly the later prophets. A theme that is developed with great beauty, power and fullness in Isaiah ch. 60. He says: 'According to some interpretations of prophecy (and I think this way myself) Isaiah's chapter as well as stanza 9 of Psalm 68 probably refers to a time still in the future when Jesus will actually reign on earth, the millennium, though there is certainly a kind of fulfillment now through Christians obedience to the Great Commission and the worldwide advance of Christianity. It is the power of God that will draw the nations of the earth to praise God.'[20]

PSALM 69

A MAN OF SORROWS

The superscription of Psalm 69 is according *'to the Lilies.'* The lilies are traditionally linked with springtime and the Passover season. They luxuriate in the valleys and grows among thorns. Nothing can be in higher contrast than the beautiful velvety softness of the lily and the thorns. The lily speaks of the purity of our Lord. On the cross they put a crown of thorns on his head and in contrast we have the lily with its perfect form, spotless purity, vivid colour and fragrant odour. Psalm 69 is associated with the lily of the valley.[1]

If David is the author of Psalm 69 it is difficult to identify the historical situation it refers to and some Biblical commentators feel we cannot identify who wrote it. As we shall see there are similarities between Psalm 22 and Psalm 69. J. Mays believes Psalm 69 clearly belongs to the exilic/postexilic period (see v 35-36) and comes from circles who in the hardships of those times persisted in 'waiting for God' and were treated with scorn. Jeremiah has often been identified with Psalm 69 as he suffered reproach from his own people. He was also zealous for God's house (Jer. 7) and was literally thrown into deep mire at the bottom of a cistern (Jer. 38).[2] J. Goldingay suggests the circumstances and attitudes in Psalm 69 also recall those of Jeremiah who was literally in danger of sinking in the mud in a cistern and who pleaded for action against his persecutors, as Nehemiah did.[3]

Psalm 69 can be divided primarily into two categories: plea in v 1, v 6, v 13-18 and v 22-29 and protest in v 7-12 and v 19-21, with a concluding confession of trust in v 30-36. Verses 7-12 portray David's commitment to the Lord and indicate his enemies are from within his own community. Verse 6 also suggests that to some extent he also represents others in the community. Vivid metaphors in Psalm 69 describe the acute danger he found himself in. Verse 2 and 13 mention *'sinking in the mire'* - v 2 and v 14 *'deep water'* - v 2 and 15 *'let not the flood sweep over me, or the deep swallow me up, or the pit close its mouth over me.'* The distressing image of being overwhelmed by water, sinking in the mire, being swallowed up by the deep or immersed by the pit, is one of being overwhelmingly close to death.

It is of interest to note if David is the author we cannot identify the period or actual situation Psalm 69 refers to as he never faced imminent death as this psalm portrays. Although the same could be said about Psalm 22. Bearing in mind he was pursued by Saul and his son Absalom rebelled against him we cannot identify a time in David's life that v 8-15 refer to. When did he become a stranger to his brethren and an alien to his mother's sons - v 8? When did he ever become a byword and the talk of those who sat at the gate of the city - v 11-12? Or when was he in such acute danger of facing death because of his enemies - v 14-15? We also cannot identify a time when v 20-28 refer to David. What was the occasion when insults broke his heart - v 20? What was the occasion when he was given poison for food and vinegar to drink? Also, we are not aware that the curse of v 22-28 ever happened to his enemies.

Along with Psalm 22 Psalm 69 is clearly a Messianic Psalm. Next to this it is the psalm most frequently quoted in the New Testament. In fact seven of its verses are directly quoted although other verses such as v 5 do not relate to Christ. The psalmist - David states that he is a servant of the Lord - v 17, 35. Moreover, that it is the Lord who has allowed him to be 'smitten' by his enemies - v 26. This is almost an echo of Psalm 22: 14, 'Thou (Lord) dost lay me in the dust of death.' A. Weiser says:

> After Psalm 22, Psalm 69 is the most quoted in the New Testament and so was interpreted in a Messianic sense as referring to Christ. Although originally the individual statements were not meant to be understood as prophecies pointing to Jesus, this deeply moving testimony to human suffering nevertheless exhibits features which are so characteristic of suffering in general, that their relation to Christ who has borne the suffering of the whole world automatically forces itself upon any serious consideration of the psalm.[4]

1-4   Save me O God! For the waters have come up to my neck. I sink in deep mire where there is no foothold: I have come into deep waters and the flood sweeps over me. I am weary with my crying: my throat is parched. My eyes grow dim with waiting for my God. More in number than the hairs of my head are those who hate me without cause: mighty are those who would destroy me, those who attack me with lies.

At the beginning of Psalm 69 there is a palpable sense of drama and desperation because of unanswered prayer concerning the psalmist's deliverance from his enemies.

From v. 3 we get the impression he has been waiting for a considerable period of time for God to answer. But, clearly God has not listened. He has not answered his prayer and he is distraught. In this respect Psalm 69: 1-3 is reminiscent of the start of Psalm 22. Also, Psalm 69: 17 says, 'Hide not your face from your servant for I am in distress, make haste to answer me.' This is reminiscent of Psalm 22: 19, 'But thou O Lord be not far off! O thou my help, hasten to my aid.' And as is the established pattern of a lament psalm, and as in Psalm 22, the psalmist goes into detail about his situation to prompt the Lord to answer his prayer. As he does so there is the temptation to think he is exaggerating the danger he is in because of his vivid images and metaphors. There may well be an element of imaginative hyperbole in this genre of lament and plea for help. As a result it is difficult to know exactly how accurate his feelings about his enemies are and the actual danger they pose to him. But, Psalm 69: 19-21 indicates both may be real: 'You know my reproach and my shame and dishonour: my foes are all known to you. Insults have broken my heart so that I am in despair. I looked for pity but there was none: and for comforters but found none. They gave me poison for food and for my thirst gave me vinegar to drink.'

Verses 1-4 focus on the suffering servant of God. 'There could scarcely be a more unnerving image of what it was like for Christ to be forsaken by his Father. Psalm 22: 1 gave him his words: these verses give a picture - a flood or worse a quicksand (mire)...*(that threaten to overwhelm him - italics mine)*. If that kind of disorientation is your nightmare, Christ has been through it before you and for you. It is v 4 that Christ actually quotes and that not on Good Friday but on Maundy Thursday in the calm before the storm. To the disciples in the upper room he explains that he will go to the cross because of those who *hate him without reason*[5] - John 15: 25: 'It is to fulfil the word that is written in their law, 'They hated me without cause.' Hebrews 5: 7 can also be seen to reflect v 1-4: 'In the days of his flesh Jesus offered up prayers and supplications with loud cries and tears *(Jesus' agony in prayer in Gethsemane)* to him who was able to save him from death and he was heard for his godly fear.'

7-12   For it is for your sake that I have borne reproach, that shame has covered my face. I have become a stranger to my brethren, an alien to my mother's sons. For zeal for your house has consumed me, and the insults of those who insult you have fallen on me. When I humbled my soul with fasting, it became my reproach. When I made sackcloth my clothing, I became a byword to them. I am the talk of those who sit in the gate, and the drunkards made songs about me.

The reproach and shame of the psalmist, God's servant, is a distinctive feature and figures prominently in Psalm 69. The clear implication in v 7 is that this happens to him because of God and on behalf of God. Reproach comes in v 7, 10 and 19, while shame comes in v 6, 7 and 19. We can identify Christ, God's suffering, sorrowful servant with the rejection, reproach and shame in this psalm. This is also poignantly mentioned in Isaiah 53: 3: 'He was despised and rejected by men: a man of sorrows and acquainted with grief: and as one from whom men hid their faces, he was despised and we esteemed him not.' Paul in Romans 15: 3 also said of Christ: 'The reproaches of those who reproached you fell on me' - an echo of Psalm 69. J. Goldingay says: 'The shame affects the attitude of the suppliant's family. The line implies more than that. The family are horrified at what they see…They disown the suppliant like a family disowning someone who has committed a terrible crime…It is the closest family, the people with whom the suppliant lives, who have turned away.'[6]

From the New Testament we can readily identify Christ with v 9: 'For zeal for your house has consumed me.' We see this in John 2 when Jesus drove out from the temple those who were selling oxen, sheep and pigeons and the money-changers. As a commentary on this we read in John 2: 17: 'Jesus' disciples remembered that it was written: 'Zeal for your house will consume me.' M. E. Tate says: 'The nature of the speaker's zealous action is unfocused, but the context suggests deep concern about the behaviour of some in the community whose actions are contrary to those appropriate for the 'house of God.'[7] Jeremiah 7 portrays God's zeal for his temple that was reflected in Jesus' action in John 2. God's own zeal found the worship of his people unacceptable. They had a false confidence in their worship expressed in the mantra 'the temple of the Lord.' Zeal indicates Jesus cared deeply and passionately for the glory of God concerning the temple and its worship and what went on in its precincts. In his concern he had the courage to confront the compromises of these practices. We may well be prudent to ask what it means to be zealous for the glory of God in our worship.

13-21   But as for me, my prayer is to you O Lord. At an acceptable time, O God, in the abundance of your steadfast love answer me. With your faithful help rescue me from sinking in the mire: let me be delivered from my enemies and from the deep waters. Let not the flood sweep over me, or the deep swallow me up, or the pit close its mouth over me. Answer me, O Lord for your steadfast love is good: according to your abundant mercy turn to me. Hide not your face from your servant: for I am in distress, make haste to answer me. Draw near to me, redeem me, set me free because of my enemies! You know my reproach and my shame and my dishonour: my foes are all known to you. Insults have broken my heart so that I am in despair. I looked for pity and there was none: and for comforters, but I found none. They gave me poison for food, and for my thirst they gave me vinegar to drink.

Psalm 69 reminds us that the Lament Psalms describe the psalmist's situation to the Lord expressing his feelings using vivid metaphors. It is as if a liturgical drama unfolds to get God's attention. Especially, as he had not yet answered prayer and from the psalmist's perspective had not listened to him. After v 13 we encounter a dramatic plea for deliverance calling upon God's steadfast love, faithfulness and abundant mercy to respond to him. There is also a note of urgency in his prayer 'make haste to help me' - v 17. His request also appeals to the Lord: 'Hide not your face from your servant.' It is as if he is establishing his right to have his prayer answered, especially as the Lord hiding his face inferred he was not with him and not listening to his prayer. God hiding his face could mean his disapproval. We can also identify the request to be saved from the deep waters, the flood and the pit, that all signify the prospect of being overwhelmed by death, with Jesus and his agony in his prayer in the garden of Gethsemane, alluded to in Hebrews 5: 7: 'In the days of his flesh, Jesus offered up prayers and supplications with loud cries and tears to him who was able to save him from death, and he was heard for his godly fear.'

In Psalm 69 the servant points out his suffering is clearly on behalf of the Lord - v 7. In v 19-21 he shares the extent of his suffering and tragedy as he recalls difficulty upon difficulty that increasingly worsens his humiliation that began in v 7. In v 20-22, 'Family solidarity essential for survival has given way to distrust and hostility. Therefore, the craving for human support, even traditional signs of sympathy, 'condolence,' 'comfort,' 'bread of pity,' have not been extended to the one in sorrow and anxiety. Social ties are broken: this is a cause for alarm and physical suffering. A vivid description of social ostracism is given in v 6-9. Treacherous friends increase the pain by their calumny.'[8] From v 7-21 as already mentioned we can identify with Christ a moving description of the sorrows and suffering of the servant in Isaiah 53: 3.

The word reproach occurs six times in Psalm 69 and twice in v 19-20. Jesus was mocked as a Prophet before the Sanhedrin; 'And some began to spit upon him, and to cover his face and to strike him saying to him, 'prophesy!' And the guards received him with blows' - Mark 14: 65. Jesus was mocked by Pilate as a King and the Roman soldiers staged a mock coronation ceremony. 'And they clothed him in a purple robe, and plaiting a crown of thorns they put it on him. And they began to salute him, 'Hail King of the Jews. And they struck his head with a reed and spat upon him and knelt down in homage to him. And when they had mocked him, they stripped him of the purple cloak, and put his own clothes on him. And they led him out to crucify him' - Mark 15: 17-20.

On the cross Jesus was also mocked as the Saviour: 'And those who passed by derided him, wagging their heads and saying: ''You who would destroy the temple and build it in three days, save yourself and come down from the cross!'' So also the chief priests mocked him to one another with the scribes saying, ''He saved others: he cannot save himself. Let the Christ, the King of Israel, come down now from the cross, that we may see and believe'' Those who were crucified with him also reviled him' - Mark 15: 29-32. Here we see that prior to his crucifixion Mark's account poignantly portrays the mockery and scorn Jesus endured for our sake and for his Father's sake. Handel's Messiah takes up the theme of Psalm 69: 20, 'Scorn has broken my heart' and very appropriately links it with the crucifixion.

Psalm 69: 21, 'for my thirst they gave me vinegar to drink' - is alluded to or quoted in each of the four Gospels in Matt. 27: 34, 48: Mark 15: 23, 36: Luke 23: 36 and John 19: 29. John's reference is the most precise because he says that Jesus was offered vinegar to drink - 'so that the Scripture would be fulfilled' - a reference to Psalm 69. 'Because of its relation to the pattern and the correspondence of the life of Jesus to it, Psalm 69 was used repeatedly in the New Testament for Christological and theological purposes. It furnished a context for reflection on Jesus' rejection by his own people - John 15: 25: on his motive in driving traders from the temple - John 3: 17: on the bitter treatment he was given instead of pity at the time of his death - John 19 and of the meaning of his suffering - Rom. 15: 3…Even the harsh prayer against the persecutors in v. 22-28…Paul found here a clue to the hardening of those in Israel who rejected Jesus - Rom. 11: 9-10. For the prophet of Revelation it pointed to the eschatological outpouring of wrath against the foes of the coming kingdom of God - Rev. 16. 1.

> Psalm 69 cannot be read directly as the prayer of Jesus or as an intentional prophecy of his suffering. But, it does provide a reflection on the passion of one who bore reproach for the sake of his God and by the way he bore it…'[9]

Verses 22-28 are indeed difficult to interpret. In the context of the Old Testament we know the psalmist in the imprecatory psalms that refer to his enemies, calls on God for vengeance, retribution and even on occasions as in Psalm 69 for their destruction. In effect it is asking for suitable punishment in return - 'For they persecute him whom you have smitten, and him whom you have wounded, they still afflict more' - v 26. There is an intensity in the request for retributive justice on enemies in the psalm that intensifies as v 22-28 unfolds. This begins with a request for their table fellowship to become a snare - for family and friends to turn against them - v 22. The psalmist then asks for serious illness - physical affliction to come upon them permanently - v 23. He compounds this with a request for God's wrath and anger to overwhelm them - v 24. His request escalates to their camp - presumably accomplices and household - being desolate and devastated, wiped out - v 25. These horrific requests become truly terrifying in v 27 - 28: 'Add to them punishment upon punishment: may they have no acquittal from you. Let them be blotted out of the book of the living: let them not be enrolled among the righteous.' 'It is to the comfort of all right thinking people that determined, destructive evil, should in the end meet its match and be itself destroyed. This is why so many of the psalms rejoice in God's coming judgement.'[10] K. Schaefer comments on v 22-28:

> The curse amounts to a request for the extinction of the family, an empty home - v 25. A strong personal faith ascribes everything that happens to God's knowledge, plan and power, even the suffering, which has incited this enemy assault - v 26. The force of the anathema demands the adversary be ex-communicated from the community of the devout - v 27-28. Retributive justice is passionately invoked.[11]

The logic of the severe punishment presumably is to match the extreme persecution his enemies inflicted upon him that almost resulted in his death. This may well be based on Exodus 21: 24: 'eye for eye, tooth for tooth.' To pray in this way was not controversial for the psalmist as God had destroyed Israel's enemies in the past. In effect the psalmist was calling on God to be the one who executed his judgement on them. What stares us in the face and startles us is how to reconcile these verses with Jesus' words of 'loving your enemies and praying for those who hate you' - Matt. 5: 43-45. 'A. Maclaren handles the seemingly incompatibility of Psalm 69 with this text saying: 'It is impossible to bring such utterances into harmony with the teachings of Jesus, and the attempt to vindicate them ignores plain facts and does violence to plain words. Better far to let them stand as a monument of the earlier stage of God's progressive revelation, and discern clearly the advance which Christian ethics has made on them.'[12] It is also possible to perceive a prophetic dimension to them the psalmist never envisaged when we see God's wrath poured out in the book of Revelation as for example in ch. 16 and 17.

29-36   But I am afflicted and in pain: let your salvation O God set me on high! I will praise the name of God with a song: I will magnify him with thanksgiving. This will please the Lord more than an ox or a bull with horns and hoofs. Let the oppressed see it and be glad: you who seek God let your hearts revive. For the Lord hears the needy, and does not despise his own that are in bonds. Let heaven and earth praise him, the seas and everything that moves in it. For God will save Zion and rebuild the cities of Judah: and his servants shall dwell there and possess it.The children of his servants shall inherit it, and those who love his name shall dwell in it.

As in Psalm 22, the last section of Psalm 69 also assumes a transition has taken place. God has heard the psalmist's prayer and rescued him from his enemies although we are not told how this happened. We must assume v 29 has taken place and salvation has come and the psalmist has been set on high - lifted up from the swirling waters of death that threatened him. As in Psalm 22, the ending of Psalm 69 bursts forth into praise and if David was the author v 33 is likely to have been the last line - because the rebuilding of the cities of Judah came from a later age than his. Verse 33 also reassures the reader that God does indeed hear the prayer of those in desperate need.

As in Psalm 22, the ending of Psalm 69 is ecstatic in its praise of God. 'In the end the poet will invite 'the seas and everything that moves in them to praise' - v 34 - how complete the rescue!Threatening waters have been tamed. The complaint is concluded with the hope for Zion, the cities of Judah and the present and future generations of the devout - v 35-36. Along with Psalm 22, this psalm is frequently quoted in the gospels in relation to Christ's suffering.'[13] In these verses we find a cosmic and an international call to praise the Lord not unlike that of the last lines in Psalm 22. 'The sufferer with his sorrow gives way to a song of praise. The singer in v 29 prays: 'Let your salvation, O God, set me up on high!' The answer to the prayer is the resurrection and ascension. The Lord is the only one of the sons of men to sing on both sides of the sea of death.'[14]

PSALM 72

THE MESSIAH'S REIGN

It is of interest to note that some well known hymns are based on Psalm 72. Isaac Watts (1672-1748) wrote 'Jesus Shall Reign' - Henry Scott Holland (1847-1917) wrote - 'Judge Eternal, Throned In Splendour' and James Montgomery (1771-1854) wrote 'Hail To The Lord's Anointed.' I am inclined to say that Psalm 72 is likely to be an obscure psalm to Christians as they are unlikely to be familiar with it. Perhaps this is because it is not quoted in the New Testament. Or, perhaps because it is not a succinct psalm one can easily remember like Psalm 23. Then again perhaps it is because it refers to Solomon and its contents appear to be outdated. Nevertheless, despite these possibilities, it is an important Messianic Psalm about the reign of Christ that demands our attention.

Psalm 72 is considered to be a Royal Psalm that was used at the coronation of a king or at the annual celebration of an enthronement. M. E. Tate in effect says that in its original context Psalm 72 is a prayer for the future realisation of the idealised hopes of the monarchy, that especially reflected the hope of Israel in exilic and post-exilic communities, for the restoration and fulfillment of the Davidic dynasty and promises related to it.[1] This psalm concludes the early collection of Davidic Psalms later incorporated into The Psalter. And the ending suggests it was read at later times as a prayer of David for his son Solomon and his descendents.

Psalm 72 is a prayer for God's blessing on the king and people and it is only one of two psalms with Solomon's name. Therefore, one interpretation is that it applies to Solomon. It is a prayer for God to establish his rule on earth through the reign of the king. The scope of the intercessions covers justice for the poor, long life for the king, prosperity, righteousness, submission from kings and nations and universal dominion. 'The present prayer asks that God participate in the policies of the crown, so that he may govern with equity, above all on behalf of the lowly and defenceless (v 2-4, 12-14).[2] J. Goldingay astutely points out the irony that during the latter part of Solomon's reign the Lord raised up adversaries from other nations against him because of his unfaithfulness. Also, because he provoked rebellion amongst those who were forced victims of his labour policies to build his palaces and Temple. In retrospect we can see the prayer of Psalm 72 was not answered for Solomon.[3]

In Psalm 72 there are five stanzas. Verses 1-4, the nature of the king's reign. Verses 5-7, the king's lengthy rule. Verses 8-11, the king's universal reign. Verses 12-14, the king's deliverance. Verses 15-17, the king's heritage. And v 18-19 are the Doxology.

1-4   Give the king your justice O God and your righteousness to the royal son! May he judge your people with righteousness and your poor with justice! Let the mountains bear prosperity for the people and the hills in righteousness! May he defend the cause of the poor of the people, give deliverance to the needy and crush the oppressor! Psalm 72 'begins with its only unequivocal prayer, that is, the only request directly put to God, containing the only invocation and the only imperative in the psalm.'[4] In this psalm the reign of the king is comprehensively described and this portrays the nature of God's kingdom on earth he seeks to establish through him. In v 1 the first petition is for God to endow the king with his justice and righteousness. These are integral attributes of God he expects his leaders to exercise. Therefore, there is a great weight of responsibility placed on the king's shoulders to uphold these qualities in his rule for the benefit of the people. In v 1-4 righteousness comes three times as this embodies the main characteristic quality of God's commandments. We learn the importance of this quality from Proverbs. 14: 34: 'Righteousness exalts a nation.' Also, it describes a descendent of David as in Jer. 23: 5-6:

> For the time is coming says the Lord, 'When I will raise up a righteous descendent from King David's line. He will be a king who rules with wisdom. He will do what is just and right throughout the land. And this will be his name: "The Lord is our righteousness."

In v 1-4 there is also an equal emphasis on justice so that the king acts on behalf of the poor and the oppressed to bring equity into their lives. The twin concepts of righteousness and justice are the very same qualities the Old Testament prophets raised when addressing the nation of Israel. A. Weiser points out that righteousness is a divine and absolute requirement of a religiously binding character. 'For behind the reign of the earthly king is God's rule as King: the righteousness of the king is a function and the mirror-image of the righteousness of God which he has promised to his people in their need for protection.'[5]

While Psalm 72 psalm may well have been composed for the inauguration of a Davidic king in Jerusalem much of the contents in its original context may refer to Solomon. But, it may also be seen as a prophecy about the coming Messiah and Christ the King. A. Weiser says, 'In the ancient church Psalm 72 was regarded as the main psalm of the Epiphany...The psalm's affinity with prophetic eschatology that seems to have encouraged the Messianic interpretation, probably originates in a common tradition of God's reign as king which was incorporated in the cultic tradition of the Covenant of Yahweh at an early date.'[6]

5-7   May the king live while the sun endures and as long as the moon throughout all generations! May he be like rain that falls on the mown grass, like showers that water the earth. In his days may righteousness flourish, and peace abound, till the moon be no more!

The second stanza is a petition for long life for the king. It is an aesthetic request using the metaphors of sun and moon that are deemed to abide for ever. There is also a poetic request for his reign to be one of prosperity for the people using the metaphors of rain and showers that make the earth fruitful. Moreover, there is a further request for righteousness to flourish during his reign and for peace - *'shalom'* to abound for ever - v 3, 7. *'Shalom'* represents more than the absence of strife or war. It signifies a complete sense of wellbeing that flows from the existence of justice and righteousness. M. E. Tate points out that although the word *'shalom'* appears only twice in this psalm, 'it brings together into a wholeness the political, economic, social and spiritual dimensions of life - which is what *'shalom'* is all about.'[7] In the New Testament we know that Christ the Messiah is the bearer of our peace - Eph. 2: 4 and our righteousness - 1 Cor. 1: 30. Christ is the one whose kingdom will have no end for it is eternal.

8-11   May the king have dominion from sea to sea, and from the River to the ends of the earth! May his foes bow before him and his enemies lick the dust! May the kings of Tarshish and of the isles render him tribute, may the kings of Sheba and Seba bring gifts! May all the kings bow down before him and all nations serve him!

Verses 8-11 are a petition for the king's universal reign. Any concern he may be a dictator or tyrant is dismissed as v 12-14 indicate he will use his authority and power to act on behalf of the poor and needy. M. Wilcox points out that the vision of an empire stretching from sea to sea and from the River Euphrates to the ends of the earth had been given to Israel at the Exodus - Exod. 23: 31. This began to take shape in the days of Solomon. Within the 'fertile crescent' which curved beyond Israel north and east to Mesopotamia and south-west to Egypt, peoples both independent and hostile (v 9) came to recognise Solomon, as well as more distant nations at the end of long journeys by sea. However, there gradually followed a long decline after his reign and this translated more readily into the hope of a reign of a future Messiah crystallised in the prayer: 'Let your kingdom come.'[8] This third stanza can also speak of Christ's universal reign and expansive kingdom. One that embraces all peoples and places that is described in Revelation 11: 15: 'The kingdom of the world has become the kingdom of our Lord and his Christ, and he will reign for ever and ever.' Psalm 72: 5-11 are eloquently captured by Isaac Watts.

> Jesus shall reign where'er the sun
> Does his successive journeys run
> His kingdom stretch from shore to shore
> Till moons shall wax and wane no more.

Psalm 72: 11 is not only seen as a prayer it was also adopted by the Christian Church as a prophecy. Because it prophesies a king greater than Solomon that was to reign a 1000 years later. The reign of Christ the Messiah.

12-14   For the king delivers the needy when he calls, the poor and him who has no helper. He has pity on the weak and the needy, and saves the lives of the needy. From oppression and violence he redeems their life: and precious in his sight is their blood.

The expansion of the king's power and territory is motivated by righteousness and compassion for the weak whom he will save. Clearly, the background to this is the compassion, the justice and righteousness of God that are integral qualities of his kingdom. James Montgomery succinctly captures the theme of v 12-14 in the second verse of his hymn: 'Hail To The Lord's anointed' that is about Christ.

> He comes with succour speedy
> To those who suffer wrong
> To help the poor and needy
> And bid the weak be strong:
> To give them songs for sighing
> Their darkness turn to light
> Whose souls condemned and dying
> Were precious in his sight.

One major characteristic quality of the ideal king and his rule and also the Messiah is their intervention on behalf of the poor amongst God's people.

15-17   Long may the king live, may gold of Sheba be given to him! May prayer be made for him continually, and blessings invoked for him all the day! May there be abundance of grain in the land: on the tops of the mountains may it wave: may its fruit last like Lebanon and may men blossom forth from the cities like the grass of the field! May his name endure for ever, his fame continue as long as the sun! May men bless themselves by him, all nations call him blessed!

These verses pronounce blessing upon blessing upon the king. The first of these superabundant blessings is for long life, followed by unceasing prayer for him all the day long. Then comes the blessing for abundant crops in the land and the increase of men in the land. Then comes the blessing on the king's name, his heritage and his fame so that they last for ever. Also men are to bless themselves by him and all nations will call him blessed. The blessing of wealth, prosperity and renown that are bestowed on the king are not only for his benefit. They are also for the benefit of his people and for other nations too. Such abundant blessings and a fruitful reign are linked to the themes that come earlier in this psalm. Those of justice and righteousness that the king is to pursue alongside helping the poor and needy. The poor and the humble are seen to be the main beneficiaries of good government by the king because they are a priority in God's eyes. 'This psalm has a special place among the psalms that speak of a Messiah who is to save the downtrodden and establish God's reign of peace and justice upon the earth.'[9]

Psalm 72 comes across as ambitious and idealistic. The cynic may claim this is unrealistic. Nations and rulers tend to use their power and wealth to dominate rather than benignly for the main benefit of the poorer nations. God is usually left out of the equation of prosperity and power and the issues of justice and righteousness are not likely to be hallmarks of the nations. P. Miller astutely says, 'Psalm 72 offers "a vision of the kingdom of God" or "a political fairy tale." In which the poor are always in the right, and the king effortlessly does the proper thing and gets the fair reward.'[10] Despite the prayer on his behalf that Psalm 72 implies Solomon received he failed to achieve the blessings it contained. But, the liturgical tradition it espouses is important because it involves God in the political struggle of the poor and weak. For in it there is found an explicit responsibility on the rulers and nations to seek justice for them. D. Kidner says, 'The New Testament nowhere quotes Psalm 72 as Messianic, but this picture of the king and his realm is so close to the prophecies of Isaiah 11: 1-5 - ('but with righteousness he shall judge the poor, and decide with equity for the meek of the earth' - v 4) and Isaiah 60-62, that if those passages are Messianic so is this.'[11] In Isaiah 61: 1-4 in his reign Christ the Messiah ministers to the poor and weak and makes them a priority. K. Schaefer goes as far as to say, 'This psalm has a special place among the psalms that speak of a Messiah who is to save the downtrodden and establish God's reign of peace and justice on the earth.'[12] We know that at the second coming of Christ when the Kingdom of God comes in all its fullness then his reign of justice and peace for the poor, needy and oppressed will be finally complete.

18-19   Blessed be the Lord, the God of Israel, who alone does wondrous things. Blessed be his glorious name for ever: may his glory fill the whole earth! Amen and Amen.

Pronouncing a blessing on the Lord and his name and that his glory may fill the earth is an appropriate ending to Psalm 72. It clearly brings into focus that all the blessings requested in prayer for the king and the people can only come from God. Blessing is also translated *worshipped* by J. Goldingay so that the emphasis in this doxology is the Lord is to be *worshipped* because only he is the bearer of these blessings. And the Lord's name is also to be *worshipped* for ever and the whole earth full of his glory. As the king pursues justice and righteousness for the poor and as God's blessing are showered upon him - in turn this points to the Lord who is also glorified and he too is blessed and worshipped. 'The king's reign and its blessing are the reflection of the sovereign rule of God and of his salvation and his fame is overshadowed by the glory of God who alone does wondrous things.'[13]

20   The prayers of David the son of Jesse are ended.
The liturgical doxology in v 18-19 marks the conclusion to the end of Book 11 of The Psalms. According to v 20 this psalm marks the last of David's prayers and also

sums up the early Davidic collection that constituted the basic content of The Psalter.

PSALM 110

A PRIEST FOR EVER

A striking feature of Psalm 110 is that David under the inspiration of the Holy Spirit is aware that he is speaking about the Messiah. By contrast in Psalm 22 he had no awareness of its relevance to Christ. There is also an unusual beginning to Psalm 110 that is unique as it contains a prophecy from God. In fact it contains two divinely inspired oracles with the second being in v 4. E. Gerstenberger points out this psalm has an abrupt beginning and the prophetic contents of the divine oracle are still more surprising. He also indicates the text of the psalm is partially obscure because of textual corruption. 'What can be made out with certainty are the two pronouncements by Yahweh (in v 1, 4) concerning an unnamed royal or messianic figure.' He also points out that divine oracles similar to those in this psalm occur in Middle Eastern cultures and elsewhere, spontaneously or by institutionalised divination. Important oracles, especially to heads of dynasties, were transmitted, modified and interpreted.[1]

The most popular setting of Psalm 110 is a royal coronation at the Temple in Jerusalem. Although it may represent only one of the traditions associated with the enthronement. The psalm may have served as the text for the installation of a king. This office represented a status that endowed him with the identity of the office and with powers. It is an Israelite adaptation of what was said to kings in the nations round about in the conduct of inaugural rituals. The appointment to priestly status in v 4 is part of the royal installation. In the traditions of kingship observed in Canaan the king was principal mediator between God and the people. Melchizedek was such a king.[2]

Psalm 110 is quoted in the New Testament more often than any other Old Testament Scripture. And on every occasion it refers to Christ. The Letters of Peter and Paul and the book of Hebrews quote Psalm 110 as does Christ himself. For example it is quoted in Matt. 22: 44, Mark 14: 62, 16: 19, Luke 22: 69, Acts 2: 34-35, 7: 55, Rom. 8: 34, Eph. 1: 20, Col. 3: 1, Heb. 1: 3, 13, 8: 1, 10: 12 and 1 Peter 3: 22. In the Early Church it was regarded as the messianic text above all others.[3] J. M. Boice considers Psalm 110 to be the greatest Messianic Psalm. It is exclusively about the Messiah with no reference to an earthly king. 'Verse 1 is quoted or alluded to at least twenty seven times and v 4 is referred to in Hebrews 5: 6, 7: 17, 21, 8: 1, 11-13 and is the dominating idea of those key chapters.'[4] A large number of scholars even refuse to associate the psalm with a Davidic king and consider it to be messianic and eschatological from the outset.[5] C. H. Spurgeon concurs and taught Psalm 110 is exclusively about Christ. David 'is not the subject of it even in the smallest degree.'[6] This train of thought appears to be somewhat enigmatic assuming these scholars believe the Messiah was to be a descendent of David.

T. Wilson points out Psalm 110 gives three magnificent pictures of Christ. Firstly, as a Priest exalted to God's right hand - v 1. Secondly, as King commanded to rule - v 2-4. Thirdly, as Judge dealing with his enemies - v 7.[7] Later Jewish belief advocated Psalm 110 was composed by David in honour of the Messiah.

1-3   The Lord says to my lord: 'Sit at my right hand, till I make your enemies your footstool.' The Lord sends forth from Zion your mighty sceptre. Rule in the midst of your foes! Your people will offer themselves freely on the day you lead your host upon the holy mountains. From the womb of the morning like dew your youth will come to you.

Psalm 110 is unique because v 1 and 3 reflect the genre of prophetic utterance that contain a speech by God. These verses reflect the divine formula characteristic of prophetic speech that is recognised by the words: 'The Lord says.' 'Each divine saying (v 1, 4) is followed by a declaration of the Lord's policy with respect to the addressee (v 2, 5-6): style and content again are characteristic of prophecy.'[8] In effect this is the highest claim to inspiration. But, in the English translation of v 1 'The Lord says to my lord' loses its impact.

> Our English language is a poor medium to transmit the majesty of the utterance. David, speaking by the Spirit, gives us a scene in the councils of the Godhead, between the Father and Son.[9]

In Hebrew the words 'The Lord speaks to my lord' are quite different. The first word for Lord is *Jehovah or Yahweh* and this is written in capital letters. It refers to the God of Israel. The second word for lord is *Adonai* and addresses a person greater than David and commands him to sit at God's right hand: and with reference to all the psalm says about sceptre and rule this is none other than Christ the Messiah.

This is a reminder that in Psalm 2 the Lord installed his Son - Christ as king on Zion his holy hill. And said to him, 'Ask of me and I will make the nations your heritage, and the ends of the earth your possession' - v 6. In Psalm 110: 1, The Lord commands Christ to 'Sit at my right hand, till I make your enemies your footstool.' In v 2 Christ is also commanded to 'Rule' over his enemies. 'The Lord sends forth from Zion your mighty scepter' - v 2, is a symbol of Christ's authority and absolute power to rule. In the Book of Hebrews after his ascension we find Christ seated at the Father's right hand on three occasions.

In 1: 3 'Christ sat down at the right hand of the Majesty on high' - after he had cleansed us from our sins. In 8: 1-2 Christ 'is seated at the right hand of the throne of the Majesty in heaven' - a minister in the true sanctuary. In 12: 2 Jesus is the pioneer and perfecter of our faith, 'who for the joy that was set before him endured the cross, despising the shame, and is seated at the right hand of the throne of God.' We also have allusions in Revelation of Christ the lamb at the throne of God in ch. 6, 7 and 14.

Of course we also know that Psalm 110: 1 is famously quoted by Christ towards the end of his ministry when the Pharisees in Matthew 22 were discussing how to catch him out by asking him questions. In this context in Matt. 22: 41-45, Jesus asked the Pharisees: 'What do you think of the Christ? Whose son is he?' They said to him, 'The son of David.' Jesus said to them, 'How is it then that David inspired by the Holy Spirit calls him Lord saying:

> The Lord said to my Lord,
> sit at my right hand, till I put
> your enemies under your feet?

If David therefore calls him Lord, how is he his son?' And no one was able to answer him a word, nor from that day did any one dare to ask him any more questions.' What appeared to be a simple question was in fact a profoundly searching one about Christ's divine origin and nature. The reason the Pharisees were silent and asked no further questions is that they believed the Messiah was descended from David and that Psalm 110 by David was about the Messiah. They knew that Christ was welcomed by the people and children as he entered Jerusalem with the shout, 'Hosanna to the Son of David' - Matt. 21: 9. They also knew that some believed that Christ was the Messiah as well. What they couldn't bring themselves to acknowledge was that Jesus was more than a descendent of David (a son of David) but that he was the Messiah -

the Son of God. If they did then they would have had to accept he was indeed the Messiah and be his disciples.

Biblical commentators point out that v 3 is one of the most difficult verses to interpret. And in v 3b-c…all the expressions are puzzling to one extent or another.[10] Verse 3 is a promise by God to the Messiah who is commanded to rule in v. 2 with the promise his people will freely offer to serve him. T. Wilson interprets those who will freely follow Christ as a Jewish remnant who will welcome him when he comes in glory to reign in the context of his Millennial reign on earth.[11] This may refer to Christ the conquering Messiah accompanied by his people in a victory parade. Regardless of how we interpret this crowd of people freely serving and worshipping Christ - the central fact is they shall be with him. There is however the heavenly host that worship God and Christ, the Messiah and Lamb at the throne of God since his ascension. And there will be people from every tribe and tongue and nation who join them who have been redeemed by Christ. The most difficult expression to translate in v 3 is 'from the womb of the dawn or morning.' This is a figurative expression representing the dawning of a perfect day.[12] C. Spurgeon points out the dew has a sparkling beauty and a freshness that speaks of the youthful vigour of those who freely give them-selves to the Lord.[13]

4-7   The Lord has sworn and will not change his mind, 'You are a priest for ever after the order of Melchizedek.' The Lord is at your right hand: he will shatter kings on the day of his wrath. He will execute judgement among the nations, filling their land with corpses: he will shatter chiefs over the wide earth. He will drink from the brook by the way: therefore, he will lift up his head.

The word of the Lord in v 4 to the Messiah is the inspired climax to Psalm 110. It discloses the unusual declaration that he is both king and priest. What stands out is that this oracle - this prophetic word of the Lord - this oath cannot be revoked because God has sworn by himself. This gives it special weight and significance.[14] 'God confirms his word, installing the king in the office of priest by means of an oath which he will not retract.'[15] This is unprecedented as even David was not both king and priest. Yet, here, the Messiah is compared to being a priest after the order of Melchizedek for ever. Three Scripture passages speak of Melchizedek – Genesis 14: 17-25, Psalm 110 and Hebrews 5-7 where he is mentioned 8 times. What stands out about him is that he was a king and a priest at the same time and in him royalty and priesthood combined.[16] What is so extra-ordinary about this prophetic declaration from God is that his oracles were addressed to a ruler descended from David whom he addresses as 'my Lord.' Two facts stand out about Melchizedek. His name means 'king of righteousness' and as king of Salem (Jerusalem) this means 'king of peace.' These two titles also appropriately describe the Messiah.

But, not only is the Messiah a priest he is also designated judge of the nations. In Mathew 25: 31-46 Jesus speaks of the Son of man coming in his glory to sit on his glorious throne and before him will be gathered all the nations for him to execute his judgement on them. K. Schaefer mentions that the second oracle has an eschatological nuance reminiscent of those of Isaiah and Zechariah. The oracle promises God's help as a warrior at the king's right hand to ensure he will be victorious against the nations and their rulers. 'Psalm 110 portrays a messianic king who perfectly embodies power that derives from God, the divine representative who will come in the full-ness of time to reign on earth. The apocalyptic movement saw the messianic victory over the nations as the climax of a drama played out in a universal context. The day of God's wrath was envisioned as the climax to world history.[17]

PSALM 118

CHIEF CORNERSTONE

Psalm 118 is the last of the Messianic Psalms. It is a processional hymn for the annual festival of the Feast of the Tabernacles or the Passover which culminated in the worshippers entering the Temple. It is set in a momentous atmosphere of celebration and thanksgiving as answered prayer for deliverance pervades it. In style, like Psalm 66, it is an Old Testament equivalent of the prayer of thanksgiving similar to that in Holy Communion. Psalm 118 is a complex and striking psalm that has a prophetic element that points to Christ.

'The ceremony in which the psalm was used took place on a particular day during the feast. It was enacted before the gates of the Temple as well as inside the Temple and seems to have reached its outward climax in a cultic dance round the altar. Among those who took part in the ceremony were the Israelite participants in the feast, the priests and 'those who fear God' - the proselytes, who are distinguished in v. 1-4 and are called upon to sing the choral songs alternatively...In v 22-25 the choir of pilgrims attending the feast joins in the praise of God.'[1] This psalm is a testimony to the Lord's goodness, stead-fast love and salvation.

Psalm 118 is the last of the Hallel Psalms. By way of reminder The Psalms of the Festival Hallel 113-118 are all to do with liberation. 'But to be saved in a spiritual sense is more than being rescued. To be 'saved' is to be rescued and transformed. And it is both rescue and transformation - salvation - that the Hallel joyously and robustly sung on the Jewish Festivals celebrates. Indeed, what these ancient psalms most remarkably express is the ecstasy of salvation, both personal and collective: the salvation of the people and nation of Israel. The very imagery of the Hallel transports us back to the Temple in

Jerusalem. If you listen closely you can almost hear the pilgrims calling for the opening of the gates and then pouring into the Temple courtyard to the sound of the Levite's cymbals, drums, trumpets and lyres and the ancient call and response that are found in Psalm 118.'[2]

The Hallel Psalms 113-117 anticipate the themes and motifs of Psalm 118. Together they provide a liturgical context for understanding Psalm 118 as Israel's thanksgiving for the steadfast love of the Lord for deliverance from death. Allusion to the Exodus reverberates throughout the psalm. We find sentences and motifs of the Song of the Sea - Exod. 15: 1-18, in the pivotal declaration, 'The Lord is my strength and my might, he has become my salvation' - along with 'the right hand of the Lord.'[3] M. Wilcock perceives the background of Psalm 118 is as complex as its structure and is rich with historical associations. In it he discerns the testimony of David the fugitive, escaping from a tight corner. 'In 2 Sam. 8 David strikes down enemy nations and this is identical to Psalm 118: 10-12. Psalm 118: 19-20 provides the background to the royal procession of 2 Sam. 6 when David brings the ark back to Jerusalem and also the Davidic Psalms 15 and 24 (Lift up your heads, O you gates…that the King of glory may come in). Moreover, in v 23, 25 and 29 we hear the prophesying of Jeremiah, full of confidence that belies his reputation for gloom. He believes the Lord will save his people and the sound of joy and gladness will once again be heard - because of the Lord's goodness and steadfast love - Jer. 33: 10-11. And this is exactly what happened when the first returning exiles laid the foundations of a new Temple - Ezra 3.11. A contemporary prophet speaks of its completion from the foundation stone to the capstone - Zech. 4: 7-9. In effect what we have in this historical background is layer upon layer, each as real and vivid as the next, combining at the Passover of 516 BC as Ezra describes it. Behind v 14-16 and 28 is the Song of Moses.'[4]

1-4   O give thanks to the Lord for he is good: his
        steadfast love endures for ever! Let Israel say,
        'His steadfast love endures for ever.' Let the
        house of Aaron say, 'His steadfast love endures
        forever.' Let those who fear the Lord say, 'His
        steadfast love endures for ever.'

In v 1 the leader in a service of royal thanksgiving
introduces a liturgical testimony to the abiding goodness
and steadfast love of God. In v 2-4 this refrain and
response is similar to that in Psalm 115: 9-11. The house
of Israel is likely to represent those who had returned
from the exile: the house of Aaron the priests and Levites,
and those who fear the Lord were those who were
religious but not Jews. The leader who has arrived with
the procession in an atmosphere of celebration and joyful
anticipation at the gates of the Temple shares his
testimony of deliverance from his enemies and is likely to
be the king.

5-9   Out of my distress I called on the Lord: he an-
        swered me and set me free. With the Lord on my
        side I do not fear. What can man do to me? The
        Lord is on my side to help me: then I shall look in
        triumph on those who hate me. It is better to take
        refuge in the Lord than to put confidence in man.
        It is better to take refuge in the Lord than to put
        confidence in princes.

The author of Psalm 118 appears to have colluded with
the king as the contents highlight how the Lord helped
him. In v 5-9 the king states his confidence in the Lord.
He also reiterates he has clearly put his faith in the Lord
and not in his army or in any princes. As this psalm was
composed in hindsight the king reflects on the period of
hostility and war and what stands out is his resolute faith
in the Lord. His confidence was not primarily in himself
or his soldiers but in his absolute trust in the Lord to give
them victory. We see evidence of his tenacious faith when

he says in v 7-8 'the Lord is on my side and it is better to take refuge in the Lord.'

Martin Luther said of Psalm 118, 'This is my psalm which I love - for truly it has deserved well of me many a time and has delivered me from many a sore affliction when neither the Emperor nor kings nor the wise nor the cunning nor the saints were able or willing to help me.' This is easily understood as the psalm is a powerful testimony to the strength of faith that flows from the direct experience of the help of God in gratitude and joyful surrender to him who is able to overcome all human afflictions and fears.[5]

10-17   All nations surrounded me: but in the name of the Lord I cut them off! They surrounded me, surrounded me on every side: in the name of the Lord I cut them off! They surrounded me like bees, they blazed like a fire of thorns: in the name of the Lord I cut them off! I was pushed hard so I was falling, but the Lord helped me. The Lord is my strength and my song and he has become my salvation. Hark, glad songs of victory in the tents of the righteous: 'The right hand of the Lord does valiantly, the right hand of the Lord is exalted, the right hand of the Lord does valiantly!' I shall not die, but live, and recount the deeds of the Lord.

The reference to 'all nations surrounded me' may relate to before the exile and to the Assyrian army in 2 Kings 18-19. In the Persian period it would refer to those who threatened the building of the Temple and the city walls by Nehemiah. While the king is speaking as if he is the only one threatened by his enemies, clearly he is speaking as a representative on behalf of God's people who were also under attack. This royal figure proceeds to testify to the Lord's salvation from Israel's enemies. In v 10-12 the king introduces a memorable liturgical refrain to capture how the Lord delivered him from the nations. In an exultant and joyful manner his faith testifies that it was 'in the name of the Lord I cut them off.' We come across this expression when David confronted Goliath in 1 Sam 17: 45 when he says: 'You come to me with a sword and with a spear and with a javelin: but I come to you in the name of the Lord of hosts...' To come in the Lord's name is to put one's faith in the Lord and to trust in his authority and power to save. A. Weiser says:

> In powerful rhythms, strengthened by the anti-thetic form of these sentences and by the hammer blows of the four times repeated refrain, the king describes his engagement with his adversary. He still trembles at the burden of those hours in which life and death hung in the balance. This accounts perhaps for the exaggerated word-pictures that on the one hand describe the threat from which there was humanly speaking no escape, but on the other hand bring into prominence against this back-ground the greatness of divine deliverance.[6]

Psalm 118 as an O. T. prayer of thanksgiving not unlike our prayers of thanksgiving in Holy Communion is a marvellous piece carefully composed and a considerable accomplishment. It may possibly rank as a literary and theological masterpiece as its superb content and structure is so impressive. The corporate responses by the various members of the congregation infuse it with an atmosphere of joyful and memorable celebration. The phrases, 'It is better to take refuge in the Lord' - 'In the name of the Lord I cut them off' and 'The right hand of the Lord does valiantly' also add a memorable dimension to it. Even the phrase, 'The Lord is my strength and my song and he has become my salvation' is a sublime truth that is indelibly etched in our minds. Also, the theme of the psalm, 'O give thanks to the Lord for he is good, his steadfast love endures for ever' is easily remembered. Viewed from this perspective, Psalm 118 is an inspirational model for our contemporary worship to emulate because if we wish to rejoice and have a celebratory style of worship, this psalm challenges our content to be full of substantial truth about the Lord. As a result, what we are singing about is memorable and remains etched in our minds and leaves us with refrains and truths we can easily recall and which strengthen our faith. While the psalmist gives some detail about his situation he consistently focuses on the Lord and praises him. It is characteristic of the king that he does not speak with presumptuous pride about victory but in humility clearly points to the Lord's goodness, steadfast love and salvation.

In v 13 the king indicates that he was pushed to the limit and almost fell, perhaps in battle but the Lord helped him. And in v 17 he alludes to the fact he shall not die but shall live, that indicates he may have come close to death. In v 15, 'Hark glad songs of victory in the tents of the righteous' may have a note of relief as well as rejoicing behind it or perhaps even an element of surprise. Perhaps, the king was expecting the Lord to keep him safe while not necessarily being victorious over his enemies.

18-25   The Lord has chastened me severely but he has not given me over to death. Open to me the gates of righteousness that I may enter through them and give thanks to the Lord. This is the gate of the Lord: the righteous will enter through it. I thank you that you have answered me and have become my salvation. The stone that the builders rejected has become the head of the corner. This is the Lord's doing and it is marvellous in our eyes. This is the day that the Lord has made: let us rejoice and be glad in it. Save us we beseech you O Lord! O Lord we beseech you give us success!

When the king says in v 18, 'The Lord has chastened me sorely, but he has not given me over to death,' this indicates again that the conflict with Israel's enemies left him feeling he might well die. Having been saved from his enemies the king can discern that through the onslaught of the enemy the Lord was disciplining and chastening his people in a very severe manner.

In God's providence the Holy Spirit inspired Psalm 118 to be composed which also had a prophetic relevance to Christ. This was a sign to him that he was the Messiah which as we shall see he recognised. Now assuming it is the king who is speaking in v 22 he either identifies himself or Israel as the stone which the builders rejected. If it was the King who was saved by the Lord from his enemies he represented the nation of small Israel - as the nation was in comparison to the might of foreign armies - had indeed experienced a marvellous salvation and victory over her enemies. Small, insignificant Israel, a little nation in contrast to her foreign enemies would have been regarded as a useless stone and one that didn't have much importance in the building block of the world stage. However, in this building analogy that likens Israel to a stone that the builders rejected she has now become the chief cornerstone. This signifies that Israel has been placed in a prominent position by the Lord. 'The chief cornerstone, an *ashlar* that has been squared has to be selected with special care, as it has to carry the weight of the building pressing on it from two directions and only good and strong material can be used for such a purpose.'[7]

> This leader of little Israel, or little Israel itself, seemed useless and was dismissed contemptuously by the nations. But, he or it turns out to occupy a more exalted position than anyone would have dreamed of. The deliverance the leader has confessed can only be seen as something extraordinary, supernatural, wonderful, in continuity with the Red Sea deliverance celebrated in the Song of Moses which the psalm echoes at other points.[8]

So wonderful was the magnificent victory over Israel's enemies that the king and the people come with hearts overflowing with gratitude and joy, praise and wonder at what the Lord has done for them. This is summed up in v 23-24, 'This is the Lord's doing and it is marvellous in our eyes. This is the day that the Lord has made: let us rejoice and be glad in it.' Clearly, and without any doubt whatsoever the Lord was responsible for their victory. In a mood of exultant joy and unrestrained pleasure the people come to the Temple to offer thanksgiving and praise and worship, to acknowledge to the Lord that their deliverance came from his hand and his right hand alone. In v 19 the deliriously happy procession of pilgrims has arrived at the Temple gates and the king shouts out: 'Open to me the gates of righteousness that I may enter through them and give thanks to the Lord. This is the gate of the Lord: the righteous shall enter through it.' Here the imagery of entering through the gates of the Temple may have a connection with Psalm 24: 7-10.

> Lift up your heads O gates! And be lifted up O ancient doors! That the king of glory may come in. Who is the king of glory? The Lord, strong and mighty, the Lord mighty in battle! Lift up your heads O gates! And be lifted up O ancient doors! That the king of glory may come in. Who is this king of glory? The Lord of hosts, he is the king of glory!

We do not know if when the king requested the gates of the Temple to be opened for him and also for the pilgrims, whether there would have been a conscious awareness of Psalm 24 - which declares that it is the Lord who is mighty in battle, something that is clearly stated in Psalm 118. But, in this psalm, as it is the king who is going to enter the gates with the pilgrims there may be an allusion to Psalm 24.

26-29   Blessed is he who enters in the name of the Lord!
        We bless you from the house of the Lord. The
        Lord is God and he has given us light. Bind up the
        festal procession of the branches, up to the horns
        of the altar.You are my God and I will praise you,
        you are my God and I will extol you.O give thanks
        to the Lord for he is good for his steadfast love
        endures for ever!

Once the king has led the congregation into the Temple
the people shout out their responses to what he has
declared and pronounce their blessing on the king
when they say: 'Blessed is he who enters in the name of
the Lord! We bless you from the house of the Lord.'
Christians have seen a messianic association with Psalm
118 and Christ, especially in v 22 that refers to the 'stone
which the builders rejected' and v 26 which proclaims a
blessing on the one who comes in the name of the Lord.
These Scripture verses are quoted in the Gospel accounts
of Palm Sunday and Passion week. Jesus himself was
familiar with the messianic associations with Psalm 118
as he identified himself as the 'stone which the builders
rejected' when he quoted v 22-23 of Psalm 118. This is
recorded in Matthew 21: 42, in Mark 12: 11 and in Luke
20: 17.

In all four Gospels Psalm 118: 26 is shouted out by the
crowds to welcome Jesus on his entry into Jerusalem and
this had a messianic association. Verses 22-23 also point
to Jesus as he was rejected but has become God's chief
cornerstone. This is acknowledged in Acts 4: 11 and in
1 Peter 2: 6. J. Mays says, 'The messianic reading of
the psalm not only supplied an identification of Jesus: it
offered in v. 22-23 an interpretive allegory of his destiny.
In his crucifixion and resurrection Jesus is the rejected
stone that has become the chief cornerstone...In the
church's liturgical use of Psalm 118, 'the day that the
Lord has made' - v 24, has become the day of rejoicing
and gladness over the resurrection of Jesus. This psalm

was associated first with Sunday as the special day of the week for Christians and then as the observance of the Christian year developed, with Easter as the special Sunday of the year. Used in this liturgical context the psalm celebrates the resurrection of Jesus as the Lord's doing, marvellous...'[9]

The six Hallel Psalms 113-117 were sung at the three great feasts, the Passover, Pentecost and the Feast of Tabernacles. At the Passover, Psalms 113 and 114 were sung before drinking the second cup of wine and the other four Psalms 115-118, were sung after the drinking of the fourth cup at the end of the ceremony. It is very likely that this was the hymn sung by our Lord and his disciples after the institution of the Lord's Supper - Matt. 26: 30. It is the only time in the Gospels we find our Lord singing. 'It is intensely interesting to study carefully the words and sentiments in the concluding paragraph of Psalm 118. It gives us an insight into the thoughts in the mind and heart of our Lord just before he went out of the upper room to Gethsemane and the cross'[10]

Psalm 118 is referred to four times in the ministry of Christ. Firstly, after his entry into Jerusalem on a colt and the foal of an ass and his public appearance in the Temple, when the crowds shouted 'Hosanna to the Son of Dave! Blessed is he that comes in the name of the Lord! Hosanna in the highest!' - Matt. 21: 1-9. Secondly, in the parable of the vineyard Jesus in Matt. 21: 42 quotes v 22-23 of Psalm 118: 'The very stone which the builders rejected has become the head of the corner. This was the Lord's doing, and it is marvellous in our eyes.' Thirdly, in Jesus' lament over Jerusalem he cried out, 'O Jerusalem, Jerusalem, killing the prophets and stoning those who are sent to you! How often would I have gathered your children together as a hen gathers her brood under her wings, and you would not! Behold your house is desolate and forsaken. For I tell you, you will not see me again until you say, 'Blessed is he who comes in the name of the Lord.' - Matt. 23: 37-39. Fourthly, in the singing of the hymn at the Lord's supper, almost certainly the closing words of the Hallel were sung, Psalm 118: 28-29: 'You are my God and I will give thanks to you: you are my God and I will extol you. O give thanks to the Lord for he is good: for his steadfast love endures for ever.'[11]

The Last Supper was undoubtedly a moving occasion for Jesus as he knew the cross lay ahead of him. Psalm 118 is likely to have reflected that solemnity as they sang, 'This is the day which the Lord has made, let us rejoice and be glad in it' - v 24. The Jewish people would have understood this as the greatest day in Israel's calendar - The Day of Atonement from Leviticus 16. It was the day when once a year the high priest entered the Holy of Holies and made atonement for the sins of the whole nation. Jesus knew that his death was to be the atonement for the sins of the world. Also, Jesus would have similarly understood Psalm 118: 27: 'Bind the festal sacrifice with branches up to the horns of the altar' as he knew that he himself was to be that sacrifice on the cross.

CHAPTER TWO

INTIMATE PSALMS

PSALM 6

THEOLOGY WITH GOD

Psalm 6 is unquestionably a fascinating psalm as there is so much more to it than at first glance meets the eye. Alongside Psalms 32, 38, 51, 102, 130 and 143, it was considered by the early church to be among the seven Penitential Psalms. When Psalm 6 was placed into this category it assumed a new emphasis and purpose. 'The shift in the function of the psalm would have begun when it was used as a congregational liturgy in Israel and was included in a book of Scripture.'[1] But, it also falls into the category of a personal lament psalm. These are noted for being emotive in their content. But, Psalm 6 numbers amongst the most emotionally and psychologically expressive. Unsurprisingly, this is of a very personal nature.

Rabbi Miriam Glazer says about Psalm 6, 'A painful, difficult psalm - difficult not to grasp intellectually, but to experience fully, emotionally. Traditional interpretations emphasise that the psalmist is describing the fear and trembling that accompanies being in the throes of physical illness...or the anguish of having to live in *galut* 'in exile' from the land of Israel.

The first section of this psalm gives such poignant expression to the experience of intense suffering that it is hard to imagine or conceive of relief coming for such an emotional abyss. For me, at least, being in pain - physical, emotional or spiritual - has often felt like that. The pain is too all encompassing: it feels as if you're closing down.'[2]

1-5   O Lord rebuke me not in your anger, nor chasten
          me in your wrath. Be gracious to me O Lord, for I
          am languishing: O Lord, heal me, for my bones
          are troubled. My soul also is sorely troubled. But
          you, O Lord - how long? Turn, O Lord save my
          life: deliver me for the sake of your steadfast love.
          For in death there is no remembrance of you: in
          Sheol who can give you praise?

Although the superscription says, 'A Psalm of David'
there is no internal evidence that links it with him. At the
same time there appears to be no historical situation that
connects it with him. Equally, no Biblical commentator
specifically links this psalm to him. On the other hand,
David may be the author who wrote this psalm but it is
not autobiographical. In his psalms that are about himself
and the Lord answers his prayer he usually ends the psalm
by either fulfilling his vows to the Lord or praising him
and testifying to his salvation in corporate worship. But,
that does not happen in Psalm 6.

This psalm is clearly a prayer for healing from physical
illness with severe emotional, physical, psychological and
spiritual symptoms. There is no reason why it should not
be considered a genuine prayer to be used by individuals
or their families on their behalf when they were suffering
from serious illness or trouble. And it may well have been
included in a formal liturgical act of worship. The psalm
opens with seven requests for God's decisive action. This
involves three kinds of assault - corporal, spiritual and
social.[3] 'This prayer for help is a passionate, agonised
appeal to the grace of God against the wrath of God…The
language of the prayer describes a person who is seriously
ill. Physical vigour wanes, body and life are disturbed,
unbalanced: groaning and grief have gone on and on and
vitality seems to leak away with the outpouring of sighs
and tears. Death seems an imminent probability.'[4] The
underlying implication of the phrase 'how long' in v 3
is that the psalmist has been praying for a considerable

time and is still waiting for the Lord to answer. This is
accentuated by v 4 that literally interpreted is: 'turn back
to me Lord.' He prays this as he is aware the Lord has
withdrawn his presence.

J. Mays touches on a key aspect of understanding Psalm 6
when he says: 'But for this prayer the theological
meaning of serious illness is even more important than
the psychological.' He also states that his prayer is 'full
of theological tensions.'[5] The psalmist perceives that his
illness and the symptoms of his body and soul have been
allowed by the Lord and that he is in his hands. This was
his way of making sense of this affliction as he perceived
there may have been a link between sin and his sickness.
This was part of Old Testament theology. But, as there
is no mention of penitence in the psalm we can assume
he is innocent of any sins or like Job is a righteous
sufferer. (By contrast in Psalm 32, 38 and 51 three of the
Penitential Psalms sin is specifically stated). What is of
particular interest is that the author does not meekly
accept these possibilities. What is of equal, if not greater
interest, is that the Lord in his silence and absence has left
him on his own to find a solution. We can sympathise
with the author as in the midst of his suffering he may
well have felt considerable confusion and concern as to
what exactly the Lord was doing.

The theological tension for him is how to resolve this
crisis. This not only involves coming to terms with why
the Lord has not answered his prayer but also making
sense of his illness, his symptoms and his feelings. His
theological dilemma is how to resolve these issues. The
Lord has clearly not answered his prayer as he is still
waiting for him to act. Therefore, his prayer is now boldly
assertive as it appeals to God's mercy and also challenges
the Lord to act as he believes he is responsible for his
crisis. We glimpse this when David says: 'Do not rebuke

me' and 'heal me' in v 1. 'Return' to me and 'deliver' me in v 2.

W. Brueggeman has some penetrating insights on Psalms 6 as a Lament Psalm. He refers to this prayer as 'the extravagance of complaint, lament, accusation, petition, indignation, assault and insistence.'[6] This is a hyperbolic and thought provoking statement. 'The psalmist's prayer boldly appeals to the Lord's faithfulness and protests against his refusal to be visibly faithful and effectively actively present in this crisis.'[7] He believes this psalm represents Israel's prayer. He insists the Lord's faith-fullness responds to need, expectation and even demand. In this context there is the psychotherapeutic importance of fully expressing hurt and rage to the Lord, with the 'unmistakable assumption' that he is not only faithful, steadfast and just - but that these attributes of the Lord are 'rightly to be mobilised on my behalf.'[8] Brueggemann also says, 'Remarkably, in the midst of this daring de-manding petition the speaker prays: 'But you, O Lord - how long?' - v 3. He points out that 'You' is the full pronoun and draws Yahweh into the situation of disorder. This is also a daring act of trust that dares to speak in terms of urgency, insistence and indignation.[9] In effect he challenges the Lord's lack of involvement.

When the psalmist says 'rebuke me not in your anger nor chasten me in your wrath' - v 1 this raises a problem as this seems to express God's incompatibility with sin.[10] Here, some Biblical commentators see that a confession of sin is explicitly implied. But, as there is no specific mention of sin or confession of it in the psalm, as there is in Psalm 32, 38 and 51, this is a speculative assumption. If we start from the premise that the psalmist is not consciously aware of any sin but still perceives the Lord has allowed his illness and his symptoms - by asking the Lord not to rebuke him in anger nor chasten him in wrath - v 1 he is stating his innocence. Although he is aware his symptoms may appear to be the result of God's anger and wrath in effect he is engaging in a theological dialogue with the Lord. He is moving beyond the traditional wisdom that advocates his suffering comes from the Lord as the direct result of his sin or that the Lord has allowed his righteous suffering. This is innovative theological ground. And it transcends the accepted boundaries of traditional wisdom. In this exploration of faith with the Lord an audacious dimension emerges. 'God who evokes and responds to lament is neither omnipotent in any conventional sense nor surrounded by docile believers. Instead, he is like a mother who dreams with this infant, that the infant may some day grow into a responsible, mature covenant partner who can enter into serious communion and conversation.'[11]

In Psalm 51: 3-4 David said: 'For I know my transgressions and my sin is ever before me. Against you, you only, have I sinned and done that which is evil in your sight, so that you are justified in your sentence and blameless in your judgment.' But, in Psalm 6, when the psalmist appears to be under God's anger and wrath, he uses an innovative theological argument when he says, 'rebuke me not in your anger, nor chasten me in your wrath.' This is an appeal to God's justice and a statement of his innocence as he refuses to recognise his symptoms are a direct result of God's anger or wrath. It is an attempt to get the Lord's attention to review his situation. He refuses to accept the traditional wisdom that his suffering is the direct result of his sin. The Lord has left him with a dilemma and his response in his covenant relationship with the Lord (where the stronger partner is obliged to help the weaker one) is to challenge the Lord's silence, his absence and his apparent refusal to answer his prayer.

In v 1 his appeal to the Lord 'not to rebuke him in anger or chasten him in wrath' is striking as it seems this is exactly what is happening. Apart from interpreting this as a statement of his innocence if for some reason he is under God's judgement perhaps he is implying 'enough is enough - things are bad enough as it is.' It is of interest to note the psalmist does not ask for help based on his innocence but on the Lord's character. His appeal for help in v 2 is based on God's graciousness and in v 4 on his steadfast love. J. M. Boice reminds us of the simple but profound truth that the psalmist calls on the name of the Lord for help, in v 1, twice in v 2, in v 3 and in v 4.[12] Despite his acute suffering and the Lord's apparent silence in not answering his prayer his faith in the Lord has remained firm. He may not comprehend why he is suffering so much nor understand why the Lord has not yet helped him, but he still expresses trust in the Lord's character by turning to him and calling on his name. It is of interest to note that in the lament psalms the author makes it a point to clearly state his situation and how he feels to the Lord although he clearly must clearly know.

Brueggemann's 'psychotherapeutic importance of fully expressing rage and hurt to the Lord' - is a deeply penetrating insight as this provides us with a key aspect of understanding many of The Psalms. In our culture we have various professionals who we can talk to and share how we feel. Of course we can also do this with friends we trust. And in contemporary worship prayer ministry is often available so we can share with other Christians how we feel and receive prayer. But, Psalm 6 reminds us that we can share how we feel now matter how distressing it is with the Lord. That is exactly what the psalmist has learned to do. He has also learned there is a therapeutic value in getting things off his chest and trusting the Lord to help him.

In v 2-3 he mentions his double agony. His bones that stand for his entire body is shaking in dismay and his heart and soul is languishing and he is thoroughly exhausted. There is 'an inner panic as well as an outer trembling.'[13] And as v 3 implies this has been going on for an agonisingly long time now. But, if the situation sounds bad it gets progressively worse. Verses 4-5 indicate that his situation is so serious the prospect of death has crossed his mind.

6-10   I am weary with my moaning: every night I flood my bed with tears: I drench my couch with my weeping. My eye wastes away because of grief, it grows weak because of all my foes. Depart from me all you workers of evil: for the Lord has heard the sound of my weeping. The Lord has heard my supplication: the Lord accepts my prayer. All my enemies shall be ashamed and sorely troubled: they shall turn back and be put to shame in a moment.

Psalm 6 may reflect the time of morning prayer when the night was still a vivid memory and the anticipation of another long night lay ahead. This may also imply the psalmist had been ill for a prolonged period of time. 'The psalmist's sickness had created both exhaustion and insomnia…The insomnia was the result partly of the pain accompanying sickness and partly the result of the spiritual anguish and sense of separation from God which resulted from that pain.'[14] The weakness of his eye compounds the state of physical decline. It implies that he has become paranoid about his enemies. Whether Psalm 6 is seen as a prayer for healing or a penitential psalm the psalmist perceives his situation worsening directly because of his enemies - v 7-8. J. Goldingay says, 'The suppliant is tired because of *ka'as*. NRSV has 'grief' but both verb and noun usually suggest rage…Perhaps the suppliant is raging because of people's attacks.'[15]

The Lament Psalms are prone to a high level of emotional intensity and the prolonged weeping of v 6 may appear exaggerated. Nevertheless, it displays an internal anguish and desperation and a monologue of intense sadness[16] -

one that is associated with the psalmist's enemies. At this late stage they appear to play a dominant part in his psychological state and plight. The focus on enemies in v 8-10 indicates a strong link between his severe physical illness with its emotional and psychological repercussions and the prospect of death in the first half of Psalm 6. 'As often occurs both in reality and The Psalms, personal suffering and enemies complicate the condition of the patient, who becomes more sensitive to hostility and rejection, even as the rivals or persons around take advantage of his or her weakness.'[17]

There is a sudden and a quite sensational transformation in Psalm 6: 8-10. A tremendous sense of relief follows as the psalmist bids his enemies to depart and to leave him alone. He unequivocally declares, the Lord has heard the sound of his weeping - 'the Lord has accepted my supplications' - 'the Lord accepts my prayer.' K. Schaefer eloquently describes this scene:

> Suddenly the poet acknowledges God's help. The description is a masterpiece. The afflicted poet spends nights in anguish, moaning and drenching the bed with tears...God intervenes and the wicked who delighted in the psalmist's humiliation are frustrated. Where does the astonishing certainty that 'the Lord has heard' come from? These words are either recited in the temple after the psalmist recovered or they are a reaction to the deliverance promised in a priestly oracle which is missing from the psalm.[18]

The psalmist's threefold testimony in v 8-9 that the Lord has at last heard his prayer clearly describes the powerful transformation that took place. Although they don't know some Biblical commentators speculate this occurred in some form of public worship. But, what they tend to overlook is the simple but profound realisation that the

Lord had answered the psalmist's prayer because he had already physically healed him!

PSALM 18

I LOVE YOU LORD

One of the things that clearly stands out in many of The Psalms is their spontaneous testimony and witness to God's glory - his goodness and salvation in the life of individuals and his people. In these psalms there is no apparent reticence nor inhibition about declaring what the Lord has done. They are bursting with irrepressible acclaim about the Lord's glory - his character and saving activity. To keep quiet about God's goodness and his salvation may well be tantamount to sin. To remain silent and not to thank the Lord about his glory and to not praise him is unthinkable. The psalmists clearly declare their thanksgiving and praise to the Lord and on occasions specifically declare this in corporate worship. There are even occasions when the psalmist wants to declare God's glory and praise to nations or to generations yet unborn! These psalms reinforce in a compelling way the place of personal testimony to the Lord in corporate worship. Bearing witness to the Lord in this way, to his character, goodness and salvation, is a powerful evangelistic witness and encourages us to have thankful hearts full of praise.

Yet, it is rare to hear testimonies in corporate worship about what the Lord has done in peoples' lives. But, on the rare occasion when this has taken place, it has been a powerful witness to God's glory and also to the faith of those who shared: and quite clearly it has been a tremendous encouragement to those listening. There are occasions when the Lord touches peoples' lives through other Christians and these can be a testimony in corporate worship to witness to God's glory and goodness. I have known the Lord touch peoples' lives in very meaningful and timely ways yet there can be a lack of personal testimony to what God has done - although I suspect this is more out of ignorance than design. Of course individuals do not necessarily have to be named who have been a channel of God's blessing to ensure the glory is given to the Lord. But, individuals should not be embarrassed to share how the Lord has ministered to them through others in the fellowship. What the Lord has done can result in glorifying him in corporate worship.

Psalm 18 vividly describes the Lord's glory, his character, goodness and salvation throughout David's life. At first glance, it may appear the Lord always rescued and saved him as soon as he asked for help: and that he was like a warrior riding on his heavenly chariot brandishing his power and sweeping his enemies from under his feet. But, this is not the way it always happened and on occasions he had to wait a considerable time before the Lord's salvation was revealed in his life. The theme of David waiting for God to answer his prayer and save him from his enemies was not a new experience for him. For example, this is seen in Psalm 22 where David distinctly voices his concern that the Lord is ignoring his plea for help and he is virtually at the mercy of his enemies. The reality is that on many occasions he prayed for help and the Lord did not answer him immediately or as quickly as he wanted. We see this in Psalm 13: 1-2: 'How long O Lord? Will you forget me forever? How long will you hide your face from me? How long shall I bear pain in my soul and have sorrow in my heart all the day? How long shall my enemy be exalted over me?' We also see David waiting for help in Psalm 40, Psalm 62, Psalm 69 and in Psalm 86, when he states he had to wait patiently for the Lord to help him. During the times when he waited for the Lord to rescue him from his enemies David's faith was tested and refined and he had to learn to be patient and trust the Lord to help him in his perfect timing. Psalm 18 reveals the Lord's glory when in God's perfect timing

David was delivered from the hands of all his enemies and from the hand of Saul.

1-3   I love you, O Lord, my strength. The Lord is my rock, and my fortress and my deliverer, my God, my rock in whom I take refuge, my shield and the horn of my salvation, my stronghold. I call upon the Lord, who is worthy to be praised, and I am saved from my enemies.

P. C. Craigie informs us that there is some degree of unanimity among scholars that Psalm 18 is ancient and a Royal Psalm to be dated in the 11th or 10th century BC. It is reasonable to suppose that the original form comes from the time of David or shortly after. It may have been used in cultic worship or one of Israel's great annual festivals.[1] Psalm 18 with 50 verses is one of the longest in The Psalter and a unique feature is the fact it can be found in 2 Samuel 22 where it is virtually identical. Although the superscription here and in 2 Samuel traditionally have David as the author Goldingay suggests there is no direct evidence for this. He believes that David's serious sins disqualify him from speaking personally in terms of his personal integrity in v 20-21 in such unequivocal terms, and it is more plausible that it was written for him and could account for the objective view of his integrity.[2] J. M. Boice on the other hand takes it at face value that David is the author and M. Wilcock says, 'Even scholars who hold *of David* does not normally mean *by David* are likely to make an exception in the case of psalm 18.'[3]

> The psalmist begins his magnificent hymn of praise with a profoundly personal statement: 'I love you.' The verb is unusual but indicates an intimacy in the relationship with God which is reflected throughout the psalm...in a series of dangerous and mortal crises. The psalmist continues by piling up a series of words and epithets in a kind of staccato style, expresses

pungently the nature of God as he has been experienced. The names reflect two themes, though each is closely related to the other: one theme is military (God is deliverer, shield and safe retreat) and the other evokes the rocky wilderness (God is cliff, stronghold and rock).[4]

In Psalm 18 David thanks the Lord for keeping him safe as the king and rescuing him from his enemies. It is a psalm forged on the tested anvil of experience. In it David glorifies God by declaring his love for the Lord and also testifying to his salvation. This is a carefully composed psalm. It is resplendent with metaphors that mirror God's glory. M. Wilcock points out that the 'Hebrew word for love is used nowhere else in the O. T. quite as it is here. The psalmist bursts out at once with his affection, even his passion, for his beloved Lord. A flood of metaphors follows, showing something of what this God means to him.'[5] Goldingay is more cool in his interpretation and says the term *raham* does not suggest intimacy so much as commitment.'[6] But, David does not indulge himself in elaborating on his love and commitment. His song of thanksgiving focuses on the Lord's glory - his character which in v 1-3 describe his saving action. Later in the psalm in v 31-32 he exalts the Lord when he says: 'Who is God, but the Lord? And who is a rock, except our God - the God who girded me with strength and made my way safe.' After this, he further elucidates at length how the Lord helped him against his enemies and strengthened him in battle.

At the same time Psalm 18 is an insight into David's faith in the Lord. On many occasions he prayed to the Lord for help against his enemies and we can discern that the Holy Spirit spoke to him about the Lord's protection by showing him images of God's glory which represented his help. While he was in the wilderness the Holy Spirit impressed on his heart that the Lord was: 'my strength' -

'my rock' - 'my fortress' - 'my deliverer' - 'my refuge' -
my shield' - 'my horn' and 'stronghold' - v 1-2. These
images of God's glory reveal the Lord's protection and
are associated in David's life with the wilderness where
he sought to escape and hide from his enemies. David
learned to tenaciously place his faith in the Lord and his
character that was as solid as the granite rocks that helped
shelter him from his enemies. M. Wilcock points out that
the '*rock* in v 2 was the cliff in the Desert of Moan. The
second *rock* (a different word) was the crags of the Wild
Goats in the desert of en Gedi. The *fortress* and the
stronghold were the caves of Adullam. All of which are
located in Israel's southern wilderness.'[7]

In v 1-3 the repeated emphasis on 'my' is a reminder
of the close personal relationship and intimacy David
had with the Lord and his reliance on him, both of which
are integral features of his psalms. In The Psalms that
have an underlying intimacy and personal knowledge of
the Lord the Lord's saving activity and character are
portrayed by his authority and majestic power that is
exercised over heaven and earth and over the kings and
rulers of the earth. We also find metaphors that capture
the Lord's activity and character which appeal to and
strengthen the imagination of faith. One of the themes that
stands out in Psalm 18 is that the Lord comes down from
the heavens to earth to help David and he manifest his
power and presence as in v 16-17: 'He reached from on
high, he took me, he drew me out of many waters. He
delivered me from my strong enemy and from those who
hated me: for they were too mighty for me.' We also read
in v 33, the Lord made my feet like hinds feet and set me
secure on the heights - implying he was out of reach of his
enemies. In v 38-49 we see David's enemies falling down
at his feet and in v 47 the Lord subdued peoples under
him.

4-19   The cords of death encompassed me, the torrents of perdition assailed me, the cords of Sheol entangled me, the snares of death confronted me. In my distress I called upon the Lord: to my God I cried for help. From his temple he heard my voice, and my cry to him reached his ears. Then the earth reeled and rocked: the foundations also of the mountains trembled and quaked because he was angry. Smoke went up from his nostrils, and devouring fire from his mouth: glowing coals flamed forth from him. He bowed the heavens and came down: thick darkness was under his feet. He rode on a cherub and flew: he came swiftly upon the wings of the wind. He made darkness his covering around him, his canopy thick clouds dark with water. Out of the brightness before him there broke through his clouds hailstones and coals of fire. The Lord also thundered in the heavens, and the Most High uttered his voice, hailstones and coals of fire. And he sent out his arrows and scattered them: he flashed forth lightnings and routed them. Then the channels of the sea were seen, and the foundations of the world were laid bare, at your rebuke O Lord, at the blast of the breath of your nostrils. He reached from on high, he took me, he drew me out of many waters. He delivered me from my strong enemy, and from those who hated me: for they were too mighty for me. They came upon me in the day of my calamity: but the Lord was my stay. He brought me into a broad place: he delivered me because he delighted in me.

David recalls the seriousness of his situation in v 3-4 when he felt that his life was in grave danger. In this distressing situation he called upon the Lord to help him - v 5. He has a vivid imagination inspired by the Holy Spirit as writing in retrospect his description of the Lord is in majestic powerful terms in comparison to his helplessness. From one perspective Psalm 18 is a complex, striking and unusual literary composition with some archaic language. The theme of God's theophany (the manifestation of God) in v 7-15 has been given cosmic dimensions achieved by the use of language which is rooted in the Near Eastern mythology but which has been transformed to express the Lord's deliverance. The Lord's divine response is depicted in language reminiscent of the Sinai theophany that was a way of expressing God's preparation for warfare in the early Hebrew poetic tradition on behalf of his servant David the king.[8] From another perspective Psalm 18 is a very personal expression of David's confidence in the Lord and his faith in him. But, this psalm is not so much about David - it is more about God's covenant faithfulness to his anointed king and his commitment and love to him and to Israel. At the same time it can also be interpreted as pointing to a future descendent of his as the messiah. But, even if David was not the author we can still readily imagine him speaking through the psalm as it accurately captures his relationship with the Lord.

In v 4-5 David in effect declares that his life is threatened and in mortal danger. He is being assailed by powerful opposing forces that seek his life and he is in distress because he might be killed. As he writes he is not just referring to one specific occasion but to the situations he found himself in on a number of occasions. But, here it is presented as the one distinct issue he faced at times as the king. After voicing his distress to the Lord and making his plea for help we can readily imagine v 6 moving smoothly onto v 16: the Lord heard his cry and reached out from on high and rescued him. But, inspired by the Holy Spirit David has had a glimpse into the heavenly places. He has been taken via the imagination of his faith into the throne room of the universe and seen that the Lord reigns, where he is worshipped night and day without ceasing by the heavenly host. God is depicted as a heavenly warrior who has authority and power over the destructive forces of nature. This is the same power that bears down on David's enemies. What then is the

significance of the manifestation of the Lord in v 7-15?
A. Weiser says:

> The particular features of the magnificent port-
> rayal of the appearance of God coming down
> from heaven, strange as they may seem to us
> on account of their archaic imagery, serve the
> purpose of illustrating - and of veiling - the awful,
> majesty and might of God.[9]

He also points out the archaic and almost mythical traits
are related to the original theophany that took place
at Sinai, rooting God's appearance with the ancient
traditions of Israel's faith.[10] The account of the Lord's
appearance reminds them in the imagination of their faith
of God's presence with them now. The Lord who is in
heaven is also the God who is with them here on earth.
This majestic powerful God who reigns in the heavenly
places does not remain distant but comes to help his
people and in this instance his anointed king. Just as when
we celebrate Communion we do this in remembrance of
Christ and are reminded of the significance of his death -
and that we too participate in his death - so too the
revelation of God linked to the theophany at Sinai is
experienced as an actual event in which God's people are
incorporated. We may discern that the Lord is described
in this manner because he was acting on behalf of his
anointed king who represents Israel. Therefore, in helping
his servant David the Lord was also acting on behalf
of Israel against her enemies. David's revelation of the
theophany of the Lord put into a new perspective his
saving activity on his behalf throughout his life. God who
was with him was the same powerful God of the Exodus.
He was also the God of his people Israel and would
continue to be the same God to David's descendents
forever. For Psalm 18 to be used in corporate worship was
like a covenant renewal between the Lord and Israel and
an affirmation of their faith in the Lord.

Although David was a hardened man of battle he learned to be reliant on the Lord from a young age when he killed Goliath. He clearly knew that his victories as the king over Israel's enemies were not just down to his fighting ability or that of his men, it was because the Lord was with him. It was the Lord who gave him victory over his enemies. Psalm 18: 31-42 vividly describes how the Lord helped David. It was the Lord who strengthened and supported him: it was the Lord who made his feet like hind's feet: it was the Lord who trained his hands for war: it was the Lord who gave him the skill to use a bow and it was the Lord who made his enemies sink under him. David had a profound trust in the Lord and he knew he was the God of his salvation and he learned to rely on the Lord. It is a reminder that the Christian life is one of continual dependence and trust in the Lord - 'Be strong in the Lord and in the strength of his might' - Eph. 6: 10. It is also a reminder that while we do not face literal enemies, our enemy is invisible, the evil one and he wages spiritual warfare against us that we may fail and be defeated as Christians. Eph. 6: 12 reminds us that we 'are not fighting against flesh and blood, but against the principalities, against the powers, against the world rulers of this present darkness, against the spiritual hosts of wickedness in the heavenly places.' Just as David learned to rely on the power and strength of the Lord to be victorious so we too have to put on the whole armour of God to stand and be victorious over the evil one.

The covenant faithfulness of God is mentioned in v 20-30 when David interprets the Lord's deliverance, protection and saving activity on his behalf, because of his faithfulness in keeping God's commandments. This was the foundation on which the covenant relationship between the Lord and his people was based, and as the Lord rewarded obedience this is why he was confident of receiving his help. Despite David's failure and sins against Uriah and Bathsheba he knew he was forgiven.

Despite this failure along with other failures during his life although not so spectacular he had been committed to the Lord since he was a young lad. His sins did not ultimately turn his heart away from the Lord to other foreign gods or idols. The reference to David's righteousness is to be seen as one that was representative of his life.

From this perspective David knew the Lord would be faithful in protecting him because of his faithfulness in being obedient. In his song of praise and thanksgiving he wants to exalt the Lord not only when God's people celebrate in corporate worship. He also wants to exalt and praise him among the nations - v 49 and he declares in v 50 that the Lord will show his steadfast love to David and to his descendents forever. His confidence is founded on God's promise to him that one of his descendents would always sit on the throne. The Lord's character and his promise to him are the basis for his confident faith in the Lord. We can conclude there is not only a close, intimate relationship portrayed in Psalm 18 between David and the Lord. There is also a tenderness and an intense bond forged between them over the years.

PSALM 23

PROTECTION AND PROVISION

Clearly and indisputably, Psalm 23 must rank as one of the best known and best loved psalms. Not only because it voices in a very personal way a confidence and trust in the Lord. But, because of its poetic beauty and imagery that powerfully touch the imagination of faith that in turn make it a memorable psalm. At first glance the sentiments of the psalm roll of the tongue with an almost naïve confidence and youthful abandon that almost suggests a carefree existence. However, behind the sentiments of Psalm 23 is a profound faith in the Lord with powerful allusions to his protection and provision. This psalm may roll off our tongue with relative ease, but, only once we have explored its imagery shall we fully appreciate its magnificent poetic power. A power that transmits faith as we comprehend on a deeper level the spiritual truths that Psalm 23 presides over.

No Biblical commentators I referred to mentioned what a striking contrast there is between the previous Psalm and Psalm 23. In Psalm 22 David's faith is stretched and tested to the limit as he struggles to comprehend why the Lord is not answering his prayer to rescue him from his enemies. The Lord allows David's faith to go to places that emotionally, psychologically and spiritually he had never been to before. He has experienced a sense of abandonment and faced in his imagination the prospect of death at the hands of his enemies. For Psalm 23 to follow with David's tranquil tones appears to present a world far removed from the sense of abandonment of Psalm 22 - and almost seems out of place as the succeeding psalm.

1-3   The Lord is my shepherd, I shall not want: he makes me to lie down in green pastures. He leads me beside still waters: he restores my soul. He leads me in paths of righteousness for his name's sake.

The opening metaphor of Psalm 23, 'The Lord is my shepherd' sets the tone for a psalm composed in this style. This metaphor is also the underlying theme that controls the imagery of the psalm. To appreciate the significance of shepherd as a metaphor for the Lord it is necessary to be aware of what this meant for David. In his culture a shepherd was an integral feature of life and a common sight although his work was of a very low rank. The shepherd had to live with the sheep twenty-four hours a day to fulfil the task of caring for them. He protected his flock from predators and provided for them by leading them to suitable pastures. He was also responsible for the sheep and accountable for their welfare. As David had been a shepherd being the youngest in his family he knew first hand what he was talking about when he spoke of the Lord as 'my shepherd.' But, J. Mays informs us that, 'In the ancient Near East the role and title of shepherd were used for leaders as a designation of their relation to the people in their charge. As a title 'shepherd' came to have specific royal connotations. God and kings were called the shepherd of their people. Both are described with rod and shepherd's crook-staff as a sign of office. In narrative, song and prophecy the Lord is called the shepherd of Israel, his flock (Gen. 49: 24, Psalm 28: 9, 74: 1, 95: 7, 100: 3, Jer. 31. 10, Micah 7: 14)…To say 'The Lord is my shepherd' invokes all the richness of this theological and political background as well as the pastoral.'[1]

P. C. Craigie points out that the metaphor of shepherd is pregnant with meaning and is not a random picture. So we can say it goes beyond the horizon of David's experience and draws on the ancient resources of the Hebrew tradition. Therefore, his use of the metaphor is linked to the broader concept of the Lord who had been the shepherd of his people over many generations. This metaphor is rich with meaning and significance as its terminology is associated with the Exodus from Egypt and the Hebrew's time in the wilderness when God provided for and protected his people. Whether it is explicit or a subtle allusion David's confidence and trust in the Lord as shepherd is linked to his saving activity in the history of his people that was the basis of their covenant faith.[2]

The use of shepherd as an image as sovereign over the people of Israel in a first person singular confession is unparalleled. It is the focus of the shepherd's care on one person that gives the psalm such intimate force.[3] The Lord as 'my shepherd' introduces the distinctive personal character of Psalm 23. It is not surprising that Christians down the centuries have identified Jesus as the 'good shepherd' in John 10 who laid down his life for the sheep - that reinforces the personal emphasis of the Lord as 'my shepherd.' But, what exactly gave David the assurance to say in such a personal way, 'My God' in Psalm 22 and 'My shepherd' in Psalm 23? What is it that enabled him to confidently have this personal relationship with the Lord? We should take care to note that these two references to the Lord by David were not quaint or sentimental images. In Psalm 22: 9-10 he clearly speaks of knowing the Lord from a very young age. And in Psalm 23 we can imagine that David as a young shepherd boy experienced God's care as his shepherd. When he says in v 3 'He leads me in paths of righteousness' - this gives us the clue for his confidence in calling God 'my shepherd.' David knew the Lord as a young man because he kept his commandments and walked in his ways. Therefore, he had an assurance of the Lord's care and protection in his life. For Christians to confidently call the Lord 'my shepherd' also demands they too walk in the Lord's commandments.

The green pastures and still waters of v 2 can refer to the provision of food, water and protection for the sheep by their shepherd. But, the main emphasis of v 2-6 can be seen as an exposition of v 1, that states because the Lord is my shepherd I shall lack nothing. The allusion in v 1-3 of the Lord's provision is that spiritually he feeds, nurtures and sustains his people. A reminder of Jesus' saying - 'I am the bread of life' - in John 7. The poetic language of these verses presents an idyllic picture of provision for the Christian. Green pastures suggests an abundance of spiritual sustenance. Still waters implies calm and rest with no concerns. He restores my soul is likely to be an allusion to spiritual renewal. To be led by the Lord in paths of righteousness refers to the Lord's guidance and is also an image of spiritual nourishment. But, this guidance is not solely for the benefit of the individual. It is for the glory of God as he shows himself to be faithful for his name's sake.

As we absorb the blessings of the remainder of Psalm 23, we may be lulled into a false sense of security that the Christian life is a carefree existence without any concerns because of the abundant provision of the Lord as a shepherd for his people. We only have to read Psalm 22 and know that this is a false conclusion or interpretation. Psalm 23 appears to represent a quite different world where such struggles of faith are alien to the psalmist's experience. How then can we reconcile these two psalms? Psalm 22 represents the struggles and trials of faith that Christians invariably will go through whatever they may turn out to be. Through them the faith of God's people is refined and stretched so that they learn to trust the Lord in a deeper manner. Psalm 23 represents God's provision and protection for his people in the overall context of their lives. And, despite facing difficulties and encountering the valley of the shadow of death God's people can be confident they will overcome them because the Lord is 'my shepherd.' The confidence of both Psalm 22 and 23 is the personal knowledge that the Lord is with the believer to nurture and protect him whatever difficulties he may encounter. 'My God, my God' in Psalm 22 and 'The Lord is my shepherd' in Psalm 23, both speak of the distinctive personal involvement of the Lord with the believer as he continues to put his trust in the Lord. But, Psalm 22 warns us that there will be times when emotionally and psychologically our faith is severely tested. This is the time when we have to be obedient to the Lord and trust him to experience his provision and protection that Psalm 23 so idyllically portrays.

4   Even though I walk through the valley of the shadow of death, I fear no evil: for you are with me: your rod and your staff comfort me.

Although the image of shepherd dominates Psalm 23 we can find three images or pictures in it. The first is that of the shepherd and the sheep - v 1-3. The second is that of the Lord as companion and the traveller - v 4 and the third is the Lord as the host and the guest - v 5-6.[4] Verse 4 clearly shows why Psalm 23 is used regularly at funeral services because of its reference to death alongside the comforting truth of God's nearness at this time. We can perceive that David's experience as a shepherd enables him to use this analogy for the Lord's presence and protection in times of danger, quite possibly from his enemies mentioned in v 5. Verse 4 is a reference to the seasonal passage from the lowlands where sheep spent the winter, through the valleys to the high pastures where they go in the summer. The valleys are places of rich pasture and water but they are also places of danger. Wild animals may lurk there and sudden floods and storms may occur. Since the sun does not shine in the valley it is a place of shadows.[5] For the Christian the valley can represent difficulties and trials and a reminder that life is not always tranquil spiritually, something we clearly see in Psalm 22. Spending time in the valley can make us apprehensive and afraid. But, the truth that David shares is that the Lord is his companion and his presence is with him, therefore he is not afraid of any danger. The comfort of the shepherd's rod and staff refers to the Lord's protection, as the rod-club fended off wild beasts and the staff-crook guided and controlled the sheep.

5-6   You prepare a table before me in the presence of my enemies: you anoint my head with oil, my cup overflows. Surely goodness and mercy shall follow me all the days of my life: and I shall dwell in the house of the Lord for ever.

Through the imagination of his faith the Lord has given David a picture that sums up his generous provision. The mention of a banquet in v 5 may have an association with a sacrificial meal in the house of God to celebrate his goodness. Or, it may be a reminder of the Passover when the Hebrews ate in haste a meal before their deliverance. Or, it may even allude to the Lord's provision for his people when they wandered in the wilderness. For Christians it may be a reminder of the Lord's Supper. Moreover, for the Lord to prepare a meal and act as host is a reminder of close fellowship with him.

Psalm 23 overflows with confidence in God's protection, provision and presence. At some particular time David has been prompted by the Holy Spirit to reflect on these things although we do not know why. But, throughout the psalm there is an accumulative confidence expressed in the Lord. From this perspective Psalm 23 can be seen as one of thanksgiving and praise to the Lord because of his faithfulness in caring for, providing for and protecting David: and also for his presence accompanying him. Thanksgiving that has its climax in v 5-6.

As David has reflected on his life and the Lord in v 5-6 he then focuses on the future with a confident expectation of the Lord's provision once again. As he thinks about his enemies who on occasions pose a real threat to his life he dismisses them with ease. They pose no concern for him. Instead, he ecstatically visualises God preparing a banquet for him at which he gives thanks and celebrates God's goodness. Verses 1-4 spoke of God's abundant provision for him in a number of ways. Now v 5-6 speak of the superabundance of the Lord's provision for the future. As he reflected on these things David has been overwhelmed by God's faithfulness and goodness. Even in the midst of possible danger due to his enemies the Lord has anointed David with the oil of gladness. And using the analogy of a banquet the Lord's provision as his host has overflowed like a cup of wine that has been filled to excess. David's confidence is compounded in v 6 when he anticipates the Lord's goodness and mercy shall be with him throughout his life. A. Weiser says:

At this very point his delight in God reaches
its climax and throws him into raptures, the
experience of the hour which he spent in the
house of God in the direct presence of the Lord
symbolically transcends the barriers of time and
space. He will dwell with God to the end of the
days and not only as his guest, but indeed as
a member of his household, that is, in a most
intimate and unbroken fellowship with God...The
hallowed atmosphere of worship is and remains
a holy experience whereby the heart feels exalted
and becomes more strongly conscious of the nearness of God...[6]

PSALM 37

FAITH FOR THE FUTURE

Along with Psalm 18, Psalm 37 is noted for being one of
the longest having 40 verses. It is also a psalm with
many images and metaphors. Another noticeable feature
is that the psalm does not use the terms 'O Lord' or 'O
God' and it not addressed to him. If this is indeed a psalm
written by David this is also a striking feature. This
is unusual for David as it does not represent a psalm
addressed to God in any personal way, although the Lord
is mentioned a number of times in it. But, it is included
as an intimate psalm because it is a challenge to have a
personal faith in the Lord, to trust him and rely on him for
provision for the future. This is clearly seen by the
exhortation to: 'trust the Lord' - v 3, to 'take delight in the
Lord' - v 4, to 'commit your way to the Lord'- v 5 and to
'be still before the Lord and wait patiently for him' - v 7.
This exhorts the righteous to have and maintain an
intimate faith and trust in the Lord in the context of their
desire for land and the wicked who possess it.

The contrast between the righteous and wicked is to be
found throughout Psalm 37. This is a theme that is also
found at the beginning of The Psalter in Psalm 1 as well

as in some of the succeeding ones and in fact in the preceding Psalm 36 as well as in Psalm 73 where under the scrutiny of the righteous the wicked prosper. The distinction between the righteous and the wicked appears an archaic one in the 21st century as we do not tend to identify with these terms or think in this mindset. But, in the psalmist's day for the community and the individual in a covenant relationship with the Lord these terms were of significance. As Psalm 37 progresses the hearer would almost certainly be reminded of Deuteronomy ch. 30. This speaks of God's blessing on the righteous and his judgement-curse on the wicked amongst his own people. In this context the extended exposition about the wicked in this psalm makes perfect sense.

Unusually, Psalm 37 is not so much identified as a psalm but more as wisdom literature similar to that of Proverbs: and it resembles more of a collection of wise sayings by an older man. In this psalm there is no petition from the righteous to resolve the issue of the wicked. Nor is it a psalm of lament or praise. Psalm 37 can be seen as a sequel to Psalm 36 and it is marked by the theological motif of the righteous possessing the land and the wicked being cut off from it (v 9: 22, 28-29, 34).[1] Also, between verses 10-22 and 28-40 there is a contrast between the righteous and the wicked. In the reference to the wicked being 'cut off' they are likely to be those within the covenant community of God's people. Whereas, in Psalm 73 concerning the wicked this is clearly not the situation.

Psalm 1 acts as an introduction to The Psalter and deals with the issue of the righteous and the wicked in a succinct way. It confidently declares that the righteous will prosper and the wicked will perish. It declares that 'blessed' - happy is the man who does not walk, nor stand, nor sit with the wicked. As you read the succeeding psalms, Psalm 1 comes across as idealistic and almost naïve, as Psalm 37 and other psalms clearly state that life is not as straightforward for the righteous as Psalm 1 says. This psalm indicates the righteous should prosper and the wicked will perish. However, in Psalm 37, the opposite is happening and God does not appear to be over-ruling matters as he is expected to. As the righteous struggle and the wicked prosper this becomes a stumbling block to their faith and also a cause of consternation and confusion about the way God orders the world. Is the Lord really in control and sovereign? Why does he allow the wicked to prosper so much, especially when they do not follow his laws and ways? Why don't the righteous automatically have a smoother path in life?

Whether or not David wrote this Psalm it reflects the faith of an older man of God that has been tried and tested over many years. As such it is a testimony to God's faithful provision and can be seen to instruct the younger disciple to have faith in God for the future and not be envious or fret because of the wicked. In other words it advocates, 'Don't be anxious, don't lose your cool, or get yourself in a state because of them.' Alternatively, it can address those who are have become bitter and whose faith has become disillusioned because of the prosperity of the wicked. J. Goldingay suggests Psalm 37 is for those who are tormented by the prosperity of the faithless. He thinks it may have been used in the monarchic period by the Judean or Ephraimite community, due to the inequalities in them that feature in the Prophets and in Nehemiah's time. As the key motif of the possession of the land would relate to a family's allocation within the promised land.[2] Another suggestion is that the audience for Psalm 37 is a community who are in a time of distress, becoming envious and fretting about the wicked.[3]

Integral to the contrast between the righteous and the wicked in Psalm 37 is the issue of land with the wicked prospering while the righteous do not have much land. In this context the righteous were aware the land that was

a gift from the Lord to his people at the conquest of
Canaan. 'The scandal to the spirit of the faithful is that the
wicked enjoy success. Power and prosperity are generated
better by autonomy than discipleship.'[4] We can concisely
say the truth Psalm 37 expresses is to trust in God's
provision for the future. This was clearly for land, as land
was the valuable commodity on which to live, grow crops
and provide pasture for animals. More land was likely to
mean bigger herds and greater prosperity. As we know,
probably around 3000 years after this psalm was written,
land in the 'Holy land' is still a precious commodity
today. Although, no commentator touches on this we
may discern an underlying issue that was also of great
significance to the righteous. Apart from being the means
of existence to occupy the land signified a place of
belonging. A place to put down roots and to have an
inheritance to pass on to one's children. But, the desire
to possess the land had in turn possessed the righteous.
The psalmist both admonishes and encourages them to
reassess their priorities and see that the Lord is their
inheritance and possession. But, the community had lost
their focus on loving the Lord and trusting him. It had
failed to put their desire for land in the correct perspective
- namely in God's hands.

1-6   Fret not yourself because of the wicked, be not
        envious of wrongdoers! For they will soon fade
        like the grass and wither like the green herb. Trust
        in the Lord and do good so you will dwell in the
        land and enjoy security. Take delight in the Lord
        and he will give you the desires of your heart.
        Commit your way to the Lord trust in him and
        he will act. He will bring forth your vindication
        as the light and your right as the noonday.

The psalmist is aware of the concern of the individual and
the community about the prosperity of the wicked and the
amount of land they have. Presumably, he has observed
this over a period of time and that it is having a negative

impact on them. He has also noted that their faith in the Lord to provide them with sufficient land for their needs has faded. Presumably, he has first hand knowledge of their disaffection, anger and resentment at the situation, and their doubts about whether the Lord is actually going to act on their behalf. K. Schaefer addresses this scenario when he says:

> The audience runs the risk of envy and destructive anger (v 1,7-8): they are bewildered by the incongruence between their faith and rough experience. Psalm 37 serves a practical purpose, to exhort the virtuous to trust God amid the manifold temptations from the behaviour of the wicked. Temptation is expressed in many ways: anger or envy, poverty or affliction, fear, doubts about God's righteousness or inconstancy.[5]

The psalmist being aware of the situation expresses his pastoral concern immediately in the opening verses of Psalm 37. He has advice he wishes to pass on to address their concerns. His opening words in v 1 admonish and confront them at the same time. The Hebrew verb for 'fret not' or do not 'be vexed' is a particularly strong one. But, fret and vexed in English do not adequately convey that the Hebrew verb *'hara'* usually refers to anger that accompanied by *'ap'* indicates blazing anger. This usually indicates hot anger turned in on oneself, because it cannot be directed towards the person it is intended.[6]

Verses 2-6 are a conditional promise and an exhortation to the righteous to fix their faith and gaze firmly onto the Lord once more. The call in v 3 is to trust the Lord and do good with the promise of dwelling in the land securely. Verse 4 reiterates this by encouraging them to take delight in the Lord, as opposed to fretting about possessing land - as he will give them their heart's desire - the land. It is a timely reminder to take delight in the Lord in their hearts as their source of joy and goodness, rather than allow it to fester with envy or fretting. In my book

'The Psalms - Intimacy, Doxology & Theology'- 2010 in the conclusion of Psalm 73 I said: 'The prosperity of the wicked and the suffering and disillusionment of the righteous pales into insignificance at the realisation that knowing the Lord encapsulates God's goodness.'[7] But, this is something that needs to be embraced in their hearts once again. Verse 5 then reinforces the promise in v 3-4 by advising them to commit their way to the Lord and trust him to act on their behalf - concerning their desire for land. To commit their way to the Lord is an act of the will turning their faith and trust into prayer. As they do so they can relinquish any negative feelings they previously had in their hearts about the wicked. A. Weiser perceptively puts his finger on the confidence and hope that trusting, delighting and committing bring.

> True confidence consists in leaving the things which are not under the control of man confidently and patiently to him who has all things in his hand.[18]

Verse 6 then compounds the truth of v 5 by stating the Lord will vindicate their heart's desire for land using the image of the light and noonday. These images reassure the hearers with further confidence and hope that the Lord will fulfil their desire for land. Their hope will be as certain as the dawning of light each new day and their confidence to inherit land will also be as consistent as the arrival of the noonday every new day. In other words, the Lord will in an overwhelmingly obvious way act on their behalf to give them the land. Verses 1-6 are a reminder of Jesus' teaching, 'Do not be anxious about your life, what you shall eat or what you shall drink, nor about your body what you shall put on…But seek first the kingdom of God and his righteousness, and all these things shall be yours as well' - Matthew 6: 25-33.

7-11   Be still before the Lord and wait patiently for him:
        fret not over him who prospers in his way, over
        the man who carries out evil devices! Refrain from
        anger and forsake wrath! Fret not yourself: it tends
        only to evil. For the wicked shall be cut off: but
        those who wait for the Lord possess the land. Yet
        a little while and the wicked will be no more:
        though you look well at his place he will not be
        there. But, the meek shall possess the land and
        delight themselves in abundant prosperity. Yet a
        little while and the wicked will be no more:
        though you look well at his place he will not be
        there. But, the meek shall possess the land and
        delight themselves in abundant prosperity.

While in v 6 the Lord will clearly act on their behalf,
there follows in v 7a the command to come before the
Lord and be still before him, to wait patiently for him to
fulfill the conditional promise given in v 2-6, as this may
not happen immediately. Verse 7b repeats v 1 and is also
a command to relinquish any negative feelings about the
wicked and their ways and a reminder of the declaration
about them in v 1.

The Biblical injunction to wait patiently for the Lord for
him to act involves submitting oneself to his sovereign
timing. This is demanding and Scripture testifies the Lord
can take considerably longer to act than we might expect
or desire. Weiser captures something of this struggle
when he speaks of the tension there exists when we have
to wait for that which we hope for but cannot yet see.
'Faith in the biblical sense requires the utmost exertion of
strength and the highest degree of activity.'[9] It may well
turn out to be the fruit of faith that is sown over the years
rather than weeks or months.

This is reflected in v 1-6 that almost seems as if the
righteous just have to passively trust the Lord to resolve
the issue of the land. But, a closer look reveals this

demands an active faith that expresses trust and reliance on the Lord in an ongoing way. This involves not fretting or being envious of the wicked and relinquishing these attitudes - v 1. This demands trusting in the Lord and doing good and walking in his ways - v 3. It requires taking delight in the Lord in their hearts - v 4. It means giving their desire for land over to the Lord - v 5. It involves committing their way to the Lord and trusting he will act - v 6. And that may take considerably longer than they would like - or we would like concerning our heart's desire. It is a call to be still before the Lord and wait patiently and prayerfully for him to act. It also means letting go of any anger or anxiety about the prosperity of the wicked - v 7. Hence, the admonition in v 8, that such anger, fret and wrath will rebound on oneself and possibly lead to evil-sin.

Here the psalmist's concern is to strengthen the faith of the individual and the community. They have become fixated with possessing the land and with the wicked and have completely lost their focus on the Lord and as a result their faith has faltered. But, in v 1 the psalmist declares the eventual demise of the wicked that will be repeated throughout the psalm. Verses 8-9 recapitulate the initial declaration in v 1 about their response to the wicked. It goes one step further in announcing the wicked will be cut off but those who wait for the Lord will possess the land. A complete reversal will take place due to the Lord's action. He will take the land away from the wicked and give it to the righteous. This can be interpreted from a liberation theology perspective. Brueggemann says: 'this reading takes the psalm (a) as a promise and guarantee of land for those who seem to have no means (except the claims of morality) whereby to acquire land, and therefore, (b) as a critical assault on present land arrangements that are unjust and that cannot be sustained. That is the psalm is turned against the wicked who now possess the very land that has been promised to 'the meek' and will indeed be given to them.'[10] We may also see a link between the meek possessing the land in v 11 and Jesus' teaching that the meek shall inherit the earth in Matthew 5: 5. While the hearers of Psalm 37 naturally hoped they would possess the land in the not too distant future, Jesus' teaching may indicate a much longer time scale and one on an eschatological level.

From v 10-11 onwards we may well discern that the Holy Spirit has inspired the psalmist to capture the thoughts of the Lord concerning the wicked and their future demise. The Lord wanted to exhort his people to trust him as being their ultimate possession and that he would always ensure they had sufficient land to provide for their needs. He wanted to reassure them that he did indeed see the integrity of how the righteous, the meek, the upright and the blameless lived, as opposed to the wicked who live without any reference to the Lord and his ways. It is likely that the righteous thought the status quo of the wicked would continue indefinitely and could see no end to it. But, in v 10 the Lord declares his perspective on the matter: 'In a little while and the wicked will be no more.' Presumably, because behind the scenes God will act even if we do not know when or how. As a result the situation will be reversed and the meek shall possess the land - presumably the land that the wicked occupied - and they shall now delight themselves in abundant prosperity. A transformation and transaction will take place concerning the land because the Lord promises it will - for those who continue to trust him and delight in him. Although no Biblical commentator suggests it we can conclude that Psalm 37 could clearly have ended at v 11, as this would have been a self-contained unit that addressed the issue of the righteous and wicked in a satisfactory way.

12-13 The wicked plots against the righteous and
       gnashes his teeth at him: but the Lord laughs at
       the wicked, for he sees that his day is coming.

Whereas in Psalm 73 Asaph on behalf of the community
voices their grievance at the prosperity of the wicked, and
how they appear to have a carefree life in contrast to the
suffering of the righteous - their grievance is not focused
on the land. It is on the truth that 'God is good to the
upright and the pure in heart' but this has not proved to
be true in their experience. So, the issue mentioned is not
one of land. But, in Psalm 37, land is the issue and the
Lord promises to resolve it in v 1-11 and the following
verses. However, as Psalm 37 progresses beyond v 12
the Lord now becomes involved in the equation about
the issue of the righteous and wicked and the possession
and dispossession of land. We see his perspective about
the righteous, the wicked and the land: along with the
Lord's saving activity on behalf of the righteous that is
described in some detail. Consequently, they are promised
to flourish whilst the wicked will eventually perish and be
cut off from the land even if at the moment they prosper.
This train of thought develops so that the Lord not only
establishes the righteous to give them and their children
an inheritance - the land, but also the wicked will lose
their land and be destroyed. The perceived injustice of the
righteous concerning the wicked and the land will be
resolved when God executes his judgement and justice on
the wicked. Psalm 37 can also be seen as a warning to the
righteous about the conditional promise of judgement for
the wicked - to encourage them to avoid taking this path
themselves.

Concerning the issue of the land Brueggemann has a
much wider perspective. He perceives the issue of the
land, 'plunges the reader immediately into practical,
public and disputed matters of property, security and
wealth, and therefore power.' They are not just elements
in sheer economic transactions but belong to the larger

fabric of communal relationships with a moral dimension, where righteousness and/or wickedness are enacted and where Yahweh's power to give or withhold blessing is operative.'[11] There is something fundamentally much bigger and more global being addressed in Psalm 37 than the concern of one community and the land. One of the things that stands out in The Psalms is the exhortation to have faith and a reliance on the Lord on an individual level as well as on a national level. As the Lord addresses the issue of the wicked in this psalm this not only refers to those the psalmist is speaking to. It also addresses the wicked on a national and international level as they do not put their trust in the Lord or follow his ways but prosper by means of injustice and wickedness. Psalm 37 clearly spells out that while the wicked may prosper there will also come a time when this will end. It may be reading too much into the text but we do well to remember that the Lord dispossessed his own people of their own land in Jerusalem when they became possessed by idolatry. We clearly see this in Jeremiah when ironically it is a foreign nation that does not follow the Lord that is used to dispossess God's people, send them into exile and cut them off from their land. The judgement that Deut. ch. 30 speaks of concerning the covenant and its blessing and curse.

In v 12 we have two powerful metaphors. The first concerns the wicked who plots against the righteous and 'gnashes' or 'grinds' their teeth at him. To 'gnash' indicates threatening action or scheming to destroy - to 'grind' them into the ground. This may well indicate the wicked have accumulated land by force or unfair means and intend to continue doing so. In the eyes of the righteous the wicked seem powerful and unassailable and think they will perpetuate their status quo. However, their plans are put into perspective in v 13 when we learn of the Lord's response. The metaphor, 'the Lord laughs' at the wicked indicates his judgement is upon them. His laughter portrays his ridicule upon their plans from the throne room of heaven. The cleverness of the wicked is thwarted by the laughter of the Lord. It is one thing when earthly enemies laugh and deride, but it is quite another issue when the Lord's laughter targets the arrogant and wicked - for he himself will actively oppose and judge them. Although the wicked are likely to prosper for a certain period of time, perhaps years - ultimately they will be on the receiving end of God's judgement.

As I write about Psalm 37 in 2010, I am aware of the financial meltdown that took place in America and Britain concerning the banks and financial institutions in the last couple of years. There was reckless lending to those who were not able to repay their loans and financial gambling as to how share prices in the future would rise or fall, or how a country's currency would also rise or fall. As a result, many individuals in these financial institutions acquired vast bonuses but almost brought these two countries to their knees. Equally, in Britain in 2010 as the Conservative and Liberal coalition government replaces the Labour one, we see how wasteful their financial expenditure was. Borrowing beyond their means with Britain inheriting a mountain of unprecedented debt. Moreover, we also see how Greece has faced a financial crisis and other countries in Europe like Spain are facing similar situations. These things highlight how individuals and nations have placed their trust in financial security that has been found wanting. I do not think it is too speculative to say the Lord may well have 'laughed' at these individuals and nations. And it may well be a sign of his judgement when these difficulties happened - as God was not included in the equation of a nation's well being. Their security solely rested on the extent of their financial resources.

The remainder of Psalm 37: 14-40 continues to portray a contrast between the righteous and the wicked. The psalmist clearly expounds that the Lord is on the side of the righteous to help him, to provide land for him, to give him and his children an inheritance and to encourage him to delight in the Lord and trust in him. The psalm also states in its closing verses the wicked shall be cut off from the land and destroyed, whereas, the righteous shall enjoy the salvation of the Lord. This is a sobering psalm which reminds us that God's justice and judgement are an inescapable fact of life. And his judgement resulting from sin will become evident sooner or later. Therefore, the righteous are exhorted to 'Wait for the Lord and keep to his way, and he will exalt you to possess the land' - v 34.

Reading in between the lines the psalmist may be calling the hearers to be content with what they have in the knowledge the Lord will always be faithful to them and provide what they need. Moreover, he calls them to be generous and openhearted to others. Psalm 37 is also a reminder that it is the Lord who gives us our wealth. This is a challenge to individuals and nations to acknowledge this and give to God generously from our finances. 1 Chronicles 29: 11-14 set in the context of God's people giving gifts to build the Temple gives us a model for doing this.

> Yours O Lord is the greatness and the power and the glory and the victory and the majesty: for all that is in the heavens and in the earth is yours: yours is the kingdom O Lord and you are exalted as head above all. Both riches and honor come from you and you rule over all. In Your hand are power and might: and in your hand it is to make great and to give strength to all. And now we thank you, our God, and praise your glorious name. But who am I and what is my people that we should be able to offer willingly? For all things come from you and of your own have we given you.

PSALM 42

THIRSTING FOR GOD

Psalms 42-43 are considered by Biblical scholars to have originally been one psalm. Psalm 42 is one of many collected by or for the director of music and is by one of the sons of Korah that are grouped together as the subsections of Books 2 and 3 of The Psalms. The Sons of Korah originated from the family of Levi. From Levi's son Kohath came Moses and his brother Aaron (and through him the hereditary priesthood) and their relative Korah who rebelled against their leadership in Numbers 16 in the journey from Egypt to Canaan. Although Korah and his family died at least one of his sons survived and later generations of the family were installed as worship leaders in Jerusalem by David. The Sons of Korah seem to have formed a guild of musicians who composed or edited another collection most of which is in Book 2 of The Psalms. The 1st Korah Collection along with the 2nd Davidic Collection and the Asaph Collection (the whole of Book 2) and the larger part of Book 3 form what is known as the 'Elohistic Psalter.'[1]

One of the best clues to the setting of Psalms 42-43 is the taunt, 'Where is your God?' 'The question is a formulaic motif used to characterise the situation in which those who trust in the Lord are put to shame in the presence of others because of some trouble that calls their faith into question.'[2] In these two psalms the enemies of God's people are clearly in mind as the antagonist. These psalms may well have been composed in the post-exilic period when God's people were at the mercy of a foreign nation. While they are seen to be a lament the depth of grief and longing they express on behalf of the community is haunting and overwhelming. They voice an inconsolable depression. A relentless mourning because of the ongoing situation they have found themselves in as there is no apparent solution to alleviate their emotional and psychological suffering. In this context the passionate desire they express for God from the depths of their very heart and soul speaks of a longing for intimacy with God that is almost unparalleled in its intensity because of the loss and pain that it springs from.

1-4   As a hart longs for flowing streams, so longs my soul for you O God. My soul thirsts for God, for the living God. When shall I come and behold the face of God? My tears have been my food day and night, while men say to me continually, 'Where is your God?' These things I remember, as I pour out my soul: how I went with the throng and led them in procession to the house of God, with glad shouts and songs of thanksgiving, a multitude keeping festival. Why are you cast down, O my soul, and why are you so disquieted within me? Hope in God: for I shall again praise him, my help and my God.

The Sons of Korah describe the peoples' plight using a simile from nature about the deer in a dry landscape longing for a drink to powerfully convey their spiritual thirst for God. Because of the circumstances of their unbearable grief and loss they have become consumed with a longing for God. Especially, for an encounter with God conveyed as beholding the face of God in his Temple in Jerusalem. Verses 1-2 move us with their pathos. Like a lover longing to embrace his long absent loved one - they powerfully and tenderly express their heartfelt desire for God. They long for the Lord's refreshing touch to satisfy their soul's desire for God. Yet their longing almost feels like a forlorn hope as their tears express that the Lord has not yet reciprocated their passionate longing. Ironically, the people who longed for a refreshing drink from the well of God have tasted instead the bitter water of their tears.[3]

6-8   My soul is cast down within me, therefore I remember you from the land of Jordan and of Hermon, from Mount Mizar. Deep calls to deep at the thunder of your cataracts: all your waves and your billows have gone over me. By day the Lord commands his steadfast love: and at night his song is with me, a prayer to the God of my life.

Verses 1-5 enable God's people to begin to voice how they feel deep within their spirits by pouring out their soul. But, this process of beginning to express their feelings and then focusing on God has to continue until a resolution is reached. Because the reality in v 6-8 is that the people are particularly depressed and despondent. They have reached a very low point and while v 1-5 offer a brief glimpse of hope they are still overwhelmed by their feelings. Now the psalmist enables the people to not only express how they feel but also to focus on God. 'Initially v 6-7 offer another expression of pain that goes behind and beyond the one in v 1-2.'[4] The metaphors that mention the land of Jordan and Mount Hermon and Mount Mizar only serve to reinforce the reality that the people are far from Jerusalem where they want to be and where God is.

A reference to Mount Hermon and the Jordan headwaters could link with the imagery of v 7. The streams that come together to form the Jordan pass through several waterfalls and cascades of crashing waters…The 'sound' of the worshipping crowd and the prospect of 'passing' on into the Temple is here replaced by the 'sound' of the crashing waters that are 'passing' over the suppliant…'The poet who desperately seeks water finds it but it is not life-giving water it is destructive.'[5]

As we read Psalm 42 we can perceive this is quite an outstanding literary composition by the Sons of Korah on behalf of God's people. They not only express how the people feel but also come up with a solution when the situation seemed insoluble to them. They express the peoples' longing for God along with their grief and also nostalgically look back and remember when they were in Jerusalem in the procession of a festival celebration that took place in the Temple. Having created this sharp contrast they then ingeniously introduce a ray of hope for the people when they write v 6 as a refrain for them. To get the people to say out aloud in v 6, 'Why are you so depressed and lacking peace? - may seem like strange psychology because they know very well why. But, this is followed by them saying: 'Hope in God for I shall again praise him, my help and my God.' In effect the people focus on the present situation and then look back at the past and then introduce hope for the future. This is an innovative dialogue of faith with the Lord and themselves to renew their faith in the Lord and their hope in him that one day they shall again praise him.

The strategy of the psalmist to look back to remember familiar landscapes is not yet successful: 'it is only the springs of chaos and despair which are released in his mind. Now the motif of water is reversed (v 2-3). He longed for water in thirst but was thinking of the waters of the ocean and those of the river, it is their waves and waterfalls that dominate his mind like one chaotic deep calling to another. He had longed for the waters of refreshment but somehow in the effort to remember God he had unleashed the primeval waters of chaos which seemed to depict so powerfully his terrible situation.'[6] But, the psalmist is not speaking personally he is speaking on behalf of God's people and voicing their acute distress. All the images of water reinforce that it is God who has been like a thunderous cataract cascading down on them and they have been submerged in his waves and billows. Metaphors that signify what the Lord's hand has allowed to happen to them. The strategy of remembering God in familiar land has resulted in a further outpouring of their feelings. But, the psalmist also recalls that in their homeland there was an assurance of God's steadfast love with his people during the day and at night, as a song of praise and thanksgiving was offered up in prayer to God because of this.

9-11   I say to God my rock: 'Why have you forgotten me? Why am I mourning because of the opp-ression of the enemy?' As with a deadly wound in my body, my adversaries taunt me, while they continually say, 'Where is your God?' Why are you cast down, O my soul, and why are you so disquieted within me? Hope in God: for I shall again praise him, my help and my God.

At the beginning of Psalm 42 the people express to God the longing of their heart's desire for communion and fellowship with him and for an intimate encounter with the face of God. As the psalm progresses they remember the wonderfully happy memories of celebrating in the Temple and experiencing the nearness of God in their homeland. At the same time they have expressed their feelings to God about their situation. Now in v 9 they bluntly address God and ask him why has he forgotten and neglected them and in effect why he has not answered their prayers. They cannot understand why God is allow-ing their enemies to continually oppress them and taunt them with the words: 'Where is your God?' They are deeply depressed and mourning because of this and also because God is not listening to them.

In v 9 they address God as their rock to remind him of the intimate relationship he had in protecting his people. As you read in between the lines of Psalm 42 when God's people tell him their enemies keep saying 'Where is your God?' - one cannot help but feel this is what God's people were also beginning to echo in their hearts. Having directly spoken to God and confronted him because of his absence and apparent neglect the people once again

speak to themselves. By addressing God in this personal
way they are seeking to rouse him into action as well as
speaking out aloud the liturgical refrain: 'Hope in God:
for I shall again praise him, my help and my God.' Not
only is this refrain directed at God but also to themselves.
To stir up their confidence and faith and their hope in
God - although there is no apparent resolution to their
presenting problem by the end of the psalm.

PSALM 43

HOPE IN THE LORD

1-2   Vindicate me O God and defend my cause against
an ungodly people: from deceitful and unjust men
deliver me! For you are the God in whom I take
refuge: why have you cast me off? Why go I
mourning because of the oppression of the enemy?

In Psalm 42 the people of God were very much turned in
on themselves because of their deep depression as they
addressed God and also themselves. But, having been
enabled to express their profound feelings to God their
hearts have been released from this introverted posture.
Now in Psalm 43 they are able to objectively reach out
beyond their subjective feelings. The transition in this
psalm is marked by the different atmosphere and mood
of the people. In comparison with the depressing tone
of Psalm 42 this psalm is positive and uplifting. P. C.
Craigie says: 'The lament of the two preceding sections of
Psalm 42 is now converted into a prayer and the form
of the transition is striking. In the lament sections the
psalmist is introverted, dwelling on memory and trying to
summon it to his aid: for practical purpose he is talking to
himself. But, now in this section of the psalm the internal
dialogue of lament is turned into an external dialogue
with God. And the change from introvertive reflection to
external plea is the beginning of real progress for the
psalmist.'[1]

'Psalm 43 provides it (Psalm 42) with resolution in the sense that here the suppliant speaks with conviction as if having won the battle with the questioning inner person expressed in the refrain...Resolution in the form of deliverance has not yet come but the suppliant can live with things better. There was no actual plea in Psalm 42 (despite v 8-9): here v 1 launches straight into plea. But the plea concerns not the suppliant's longing to be able to get back to Jerusalem to see God, nor the scornful questions, nor God's own abandonment: instead the plea concerns the enemy who makes that return both desirable and impossible...Solve this problem and all others will be solved. The plea works with a legal framework suggesting God seated in the court in the heavens: that is the nature of a 'plea.' We know from 42: 9 that the suppliant feels in the right over against the enemy.'[2]

A. Weiser eloquently describes the change in the peoples' heart and mind that has occurred in Psalm 43 although he only refers to the individual. 'The struggle of his soul against the doubts by which he had been seized has enabled the worshipper to reach the stage where he is able to pass victoriously through the darkness of his suffering until he has risen to the sure knowledge that his prayer has been granted.'[3]

3-4   O send out your light and your truth: let them lead me, let them bring me to your holy hill and to your dwelling! Then I will go to the altar of God, to God my exceeding joy: and I will praise you with the lyre, O God, my God.

Verses 1-2 indicate a new found confidence in God to defend and deliver his people from their enemies. In anticipation of God's salvation his people can now see with the imagination of faith the real possibility of returning to Jerusalem and worshipping God in the Temple. Because of the darkness of their soul due to their enemies the people now astutely pray for God's light and truth to lead them out of this darkness and to the Temple in Jerusalem. The taunt of, 'Where is your God?' was a deceitful truth of their enemies that oppressed them and sent them into a deep depression. The truth of God's love and faithfulness and deliverance is the light that will dispel the deceit of this darkness. They will not only be set free in their hearts and minds but also be set free to come to the altar of God - to be with God their exceeding joy. The communion, fellowship and intimacy with God they fervently desired in Psalm 42, but which seemed so elusive, is now becoming through the imagination of faith a tangible reality before their very eyes.

5   Why are you so cast down, O my soul, and why are you so disquieted within me? Hope in God: for I shall again praise him, my help and my God.

In the surge of their new found confidence and faith in God that he has heard their prayer and will at some time in the future enable them to return to Jerusalem it seems somewhat surprising that Psalm 43 should end on the refrain which was a dominant feature of Psalm 42. Then again perhaps it is not surprising as in this context of assurance of answered prayer this refrain no longer has any hold on them and they have been released from it. Now that they have been set free from their deep depression that the first half of this refrain expressed - they can embrace with confidence the hope the second half of this refrain expressed, but which was not yet a tangible reality in Psalm 42. 'What touches our hearts here is not only the high artistic quality of the psalm inherent in the life-like and deeply felt portrayal of the struggle which took place in the psalmist's soul *(and the peoples' soul - italics mine):* the way in which here man's longing for God is shown to be a power which sustains him through fear and torment, doubt and temptation, till he overcomes them by faith and by his waiting for God, is even today still able to bring comfort and help to troubled souls...'[4]

Here, we do well to remember that it is the Lord who gies us the desire to experience that communion, fellowship and intimacy with him either on our own or with others in the context of corporate worship. As we respond to the initiative of the Holy Spirit to draw us close to God and Christ - Psalms 42-43 teach us that there will be occasions of great difficulty, oppression or serious trouble when we need a tenacious faith to reach out to God to lead us to himself. So that in his perfect timing he will save us from the situation that might overwhelm us and our faith.

PSALM 63

LONGING FOR GOD

In Psalm 63 I am inclined to think that the Holy Spirit was giving David the longing for God. The longing for communion with him and the desire to be in his presence in corporate worship in Jerusalem. His heart's desire is understandable as he was in the wilderness and had not been able to worship at Jerusalem for some time.

Psalm 63 contains two important truths and the first we have already touched on. Namely, that our longing for God comes from God himself. This is a desire he continually gives us - the ongoing longing for communion with himself. Although some of the psalms like 42 and 43 and other Lament Psalms feel as if the Lord has left the believer or his people on their own to tenaciously seek after him for help or to encounter him. The second truth is that the Lord wants us to have an expectation that we shall powerfully encounter him and Christ and his love in corporate worship. The intimate longing for God is complemented by the desire to pray we will encounter the Lord in a profound way in our corporate worship. But, we can feel condemned or guilty or inadequate because our longing for God does not match that of Psalm 63. However, if we pursue the truth of this psalm, the striking thing about this train of thought is that it speaks to us about praise and worship being the overflow of a heart that has had a rich encounter with God and Christ. To deepen our corporate praise and worship a good place to start is to ask the Holy Spirit to bring us into a fresh encounter with God and Christ that fills our hearts in a new way with their love. So that our souls may be filled with a new outpouring of praise and worship.

1-4   O God, you are my God, I seek you, my soul thirsts for you: my flesh faints for you, as in a dry and weary land where no water is. So I have looked upon you in the sanctuary, beholding your power and glory. Because your steadfast love is better than life, my lips will praise you. So I will bless you as long as I live: I will lift up my hands and call on your name.

Psalm 63 is attributed to David when he was in the wilderness of Judah. Either this refers to the time when Saul sought to kill him or when he was fleeing from his son Absalom who sought to kill him. But, as David speaks of himself as the king we can assume it concerns Absalom. Some Biblical commentators are quite taken with this psalm as it expresses David's acute longing for God and his presence and which is also a testimony of praise to God's love and protection. Here are two examples of what they say: 'There may be other songs that equal this outpouring of devotion: but there are few if any that surpass it.' 'This is unquestionably one of the most beautiful and touching psalms in the whole Psalter.'[1]

The emphasis on seeking or searching for the Lord in v 1 is reminiscent of Psalm 27: 4, 7. There in the context of his enemies the one thing David has asked of the Lord and which he will seek after is, 'to dwell in the house of the Lord.' It is not reading too much into the interpretation of Psalm 63: 1 to imagine that David had in mind God's commandment to seek him as he had done in

Psalm 27. But, as he could not literally go to Jerusalem to encounter the Lord he takes this opportunity to share his deepest longing for him, as if to say: *'I don't need to be commanded to do this. Lord this is how I really feel deep within my spirit.'*

> The verb and at least some of those later ones describe aspects of the ongoing dynamic of the author's life with God, and v 1 refers not to a onetime present searching that has not reached what it is looking for, but to an aspect of an ongoing pattern of life with God. That life involves searching, thirsting, fainting, bringing to mind, muttering and cleaving. But, it also involves looking, seeing, being filled, being supported, being delivered. And, further, it therefore also involves glorifying, worshipping, lifting hands, resounding, praising, rejoicing and exulting...It is a psalm of trust that presupposes experiences of God's deliverance, but does not issue from one such experience.[2]

If David is in the wilderness it is reasonable to assume he has been there for some time and while he is concerned about his enemies his greater concern is his desire to return to Jerusalem and to be in God's presence to worship him and encounter him once again. We can be fairly certain of this because of his reference in v 2 of having met with God in the past in the sanctuary in Jerusalem. Although there is an implicit trust in Psalm 63 for the Lord to satisfy David's longing for him to some extent I am inclined to disagree with Goldingay that this is essentially a psalm of trust. The essence of Psalm 63 is David's longing for God - v 1. His desire to experience God again - v 2 and his desire to worship God in the future - v 3. To appreciate the intensity of this longing we must remember that he had been in the wilderness for some time now fleeing from his son Absalom and it must have been quite some time since he had been able to worship the Lord in Jerusalem. So while there is indeed an underlying confidence and trust in God expressed in v 7-8 I am inclined to interpret Psalm 63 as a prayer of profound longing for God marked with joyful praise - as having expressed his heartfelt longing for God David is reliant on him to fulfill it.

It is striking to compare Psalm 63 with Psalm 42 and 43 where the psalmist also longs for God although there is a clear contrast between them. In Psalm 42 the people of God long for God because of the oppression of their enemies in exile and because they are deeply depressed. It takes until the middle of Psalm 43 before they are able to envisage praising the Lord and worshipping him. But, in Psalm 63 despite enemies being in the background the atmosphere is eloquently uplifting. Here, David's enemies are almost a footnote in the text. Equally, his emotional and mental equilibrium is surprisingly upbeat, considering the number of psalms he composed about his enemies where he feels acutely vulnerable and emotionally and psychologically desperate. In this context Psalm 63 is unusual as it does not adhere to the usual pattern of David's psalms about his enemies. So it is difficult to reconcile David's joyful confidence in the Lord with his enemies in the background. It just doesn't fit the normal pattern of his psalms for deliverance from his enemies and is not characteristic of them. This can be seen again if we compare Psalm 63 with Psalm 64 where the issue of David's enemies preoccupies him considerably more and does not match the joyful and uplifting tone of Psalm 63.

I wonder as David thought about Absalom pursuing him if he also thought about how much he missed being in Jerusalem the place he associated with God's presence and where he was able to worship? What predominantly troubled him was his absence from Jerusalem because he missed God's presence there. As he reflects on this he realises just how much he is missing the Lord in the context of worship. His soul is spiritually dry and being in the arid wilderness provides an appropriate metaphor for expressing his longing for God. As David dwelt on his acute longing for God I am inclined to think the Holy Spirit gave him the assurance that he was safe from his enemies and that in due course he would return to Jerusalem. This is likely to account for the joyful and uplifting nature of Psalm 63. Moreover, I am inclined to think that the Holy Spirit also reminded David of the occasions when he had been in God's presence in Jerusalem and as he remembered those times he was inspired to write v 2-8. A. Weiser captures just how special this recollection or revelation was:

> It is only against the background of the worship-per's ardent yearning for the presence of God that the experience which fills his heart with joy and gratitude to God is clearly set off in all its magnitude...the word so (v 2) means that as his soul thirsted for God and longed for him, he was allowed to behold him...so completely does it (God's *hesed*-love) take hold of his heart that his lips cannot help praising God, bearing witness to the things with which his heart is full.[3]

Whether beholding the Lord and encountering him in-volved looking back or whether it was a revelation like that of Isaiah 6 God has responded to David's longing by flooding his heart and soul with his loving kindness. A number of years ago I wrote about the Lord and said: 'What can compare or compete with your presence within me?' that was a sign of his love. As David thought of the sanctuary in Jerusalem God came to him in the wilderness and he was now immersed in the Lord's presence. That experience of communion with God was a reminder of just how satisfying knowing the Lord was. From that perspective it was not an exaggeration for David to say, 'your loving kindness is better than life.' At that moment the Lord abundantly answered his prayer and bathed him in his love and presence. In the difficult situation he was in he discovered in a new way the consolation of God's loving kindness   to satisfy his soul. As a result his heart is now bursting and overflowing with praise at having been renewed spiritually by the Lord. Now he cannot but praise the Lord and bless him as long as he lives and lift up his hands and call on his name. G. von Rad calls this encounter with   the Lord - 'a retreat into the realm of the most sublime communion with God.'[4]

5-8   My soul is feasted as with marrow and fat and my mouth praises you with joyful lips, when I think of you upon my bed, and meditate on you in the watches of the night: for you have been my help and in the shadow of your wings I sing for joy. My soul clings to you: your right hand upholds me.

In Psalm 36: 7-8 David similarly says: 'How precious is your steadfast love O God! The children of men take refuge in the shadow of your wings. They feast on the abundance of your house...' The reference to eating may have involved offering a sacrifice to the Lord in worship where half was eaten as a communal meal.[33] This also symbolises the spiritual nourishment of an encounter with the Lord. The mention of the shadow of your wings may refer to the wings of the cherubim on the throne of God in the Holy of Holies that signifies finding protection at the heart of God's powerful presence. Verses 4 and 5-8 are David's response to having encountered the Lord as he ecstatically declares his love and commitment to him. Verse 6 that speaks of meditating on the Lord at night upon his bed is a clear indication that he has already had what amounts to a life-changing encounter with the Lord in the wilderness. David may have assumed the Lord was going to answer his prayer for his longing for God when he was able to return to Jerusalem. But, it appears the Lord has unexpectedly met with him in the wilderness. So he will bless the Lord as long as he lives: he will lift up his hands and call on his name: he will praise him with joyful lips: he will sing for joy in the shadow of his wings and he will cling to him. These are ardent declarations of commitment, love and worship to the Lord and an insight into the intimacy between the Lord and David.

Verses 9-10 are as has already been mentioned about David's enemies who are almost a footnote in this psalm. They are mentioned and dealt with in the briefest manner we encounter in The Psalms. Their defeat and destruction is concisely stated in two succinct verses of Scripture. Then in v 11 David the king rejoices in God alongside all those who swear-call on the Lord while his enemies will be silenced. David's enemies are relegated to the realm of a footnote and the fact that he has not had to spend half the psalm asking for deliverance from them because he is not feeling acutely vulnerable is unusually striking.

PSALM 84

A JOYFUL HEART

Psalms 84-89 are designated the 2nd Korah Collection although only 4 are attributed to it. Psalm 84 marks the point in Book 3 of The Psalms that reverts to the practice of Book 1 in using the name Yahweh - the Lord, (The Psalms in Book 2 have used Elohim - God). In Book 3 two of the three Korah Psalms appear to run parallel to those at the beginning of Book 2. It is possible we have been left with two alternative liturgies in two different idioms.[1] Psalm 84 celebrates Zion and its Temple as God's dwelling place. 'Its joy in the place where God dwells and the comparisons and experiences used to illustrate that joy make it a highly expressive poem.'[2] (Psalms 46, 48 and 76 are also Zion Psalms). Although the speaker in Psalm 84 is an individual it was likely to have been sung at some stage in a procession on the way to the Temple by those who were on a pilgrimage to

Jerusalem for a major festival. As Psalm 84 is not strictly listed amongst the Pilgrimage Psalms 120-134 one of its distinctive features is its concern with the relationship between a pilgrimage to the Temple and the reality of life separated from it when one returns home.[3]

1-4   How lovely is your dwelling place, O Lord of Hosts! My soul longs, yes, faints for the courts of the Lord: my heart and flesh sing for joy to the living God. Even the sparrow finds a home and the swallow a nest for herself, where she may lay her young at your altars, O Lord of hosts, my king and my God. Blessed are those who dwell in your house, ever singing your praise!

Psalm 84 is an inspiring, joyful and uplifting psalm that was probably sung by pilgrims on their way to the Temple in Jerusalem to worship God. The anticipation of worshipping the Lord and encountering his presence reflects that this was a tremendous privilege for those on their pilgrimage. J. M. Boice offers another interpretation alongside this one. In 1 Chron. 24-26 the sons of Levi are assigned to various places of service in the Lord's house. Aaron was of this tribe and his sons were divided into twenty-four groups to maintain the sacrifices at the altar - 1 Chron. 24. The descendents of Aaron's cousins Asaph, Heman and Jeduthan were divided into smaller groups to conduct the music accompanied by harps, lyres and cymbals - 1 Chron. 25.

In 1 Chron. 26 there is a record of the assignments given to a third branch of Levi's tribe who were the Sons of Korah. They were chosen to be gatekeepers and this was humble work that required strength. Boice suggests it is the Sons of Korah who wrote Psalm 84 and that v 1-4 and v 10 specifically refer to them with v 5-7 referring to those on pilgrimage.[4] But, both the gatekeepers and pilgrims could have been identified with v 1-4. From the perspective of the Sons of Korah the observations about the sparrow and the swallow may have come from them. In the O. T. the sparrow was worth virtually nothing yet it found a home near God's altar. While the swallow is symbolic of restlessness as it is always flying from dawn to dusk when it is time to mate it builds its nest in the Temple and settles on it to raise her young.

In Psalm 84 there is a distinct emphasis on the Lord's dwelling place, on the altars of the Lord, the courts of the Lord and the house of God and the ecstatic joy that comes from being in the Temple and being in God's presence. 'My heart and flesh sing for joy to the living God' - expresses the overwhelming joy of arriving at the Temple in Jerusalem, of worshipping and also encountering God. The psalm is deeply moving and has intimately tender notes to express the festal joy of celebration.[5] When the pilgrims sing, 'How lovely' in v 1 the translation refers to something or someone who is 'beloved.' The double emphasis in this context may refer to both the Temple and the Lord whom they love. The correct translation in v 2 for 'long' is the Hebrew verb for 'craved' *(kasap)* which is very rare. Also in v 2 the Hebrew translation for 'faints' is 'exhausted itself.' 'Both *(craved and exhausted)* are forceful in meaning, the more so in combination. The first suggests greed, keenness or desperation. The second implies the person is consumed by this feeling. Together they suggest the person was torn apart by this longing…In the context it makes sense to take these verbs to refer to the intense, consuming longing the pilgrims felt in looking forward to coming into Yahweh's courtyards.'[6]

As I studied Psalm 84 along with those in which God's people eagerly anticipate worshipping the Lord I have been struck by how special these occasions were for them and what a privilege they must have felt: and what treasured memories they stored up to recall in the future. These psalms are a reminder of the tremendous privilege we have in worshipping the Lord. They challenge us about how we come to worship the Lord on Sundays and how special God's house should be to us and about how we conduct our worship. Verses 1-2 express the pilgrims' intense longing and eager anticipation and joy of arriving at the Temple in Jerusalem: and v 3-4 capture just how special a privilege they felt it was for those who were regularly involved in the worship there. Weiser captures the special atmosphere and the memorable impression the Temple and worship made on the pilgrims. 'The sight of the Temple draws from the pilgrim a cry of deep joy. The song of rejoicing which he raises to the glory of God is resonant not only with the tremendous impression Solomon's magnificent building makes upon him, but much more still with his gratitude and joy that his yearning has been fulfilled. He accepts the bliss of being able to take part in the worship of the Temple as a gift from God's hand. It is hardly possible to imagine what the divine service that as layman he could attend only in the forecourt of the Temple may have meant to this man, who can say of himself that he was consumed with such yearning for the forecourts of Yahweh that he was pining away!...the whole man, 'heart and flesh' breaks into a sudden shout of joy as soon as he becomes fully and almost physically aware that God is near him in the Temple.'[7]

5-7   Blessed are the men whose strength is in you in whose hearts are the highways to Zion. As they go through the valley of Baca they make it a place of springs: the early rain also covers it with pools. They go from strength to strength: the God of gods will be seen in Zion.

Verse 4 could imply that the Levites and priests in Jerusalem had a far greater blessing and privilege in being involved in the worship at the Temple than the pilgrims whose visits may have been rare. However, this is countered by v 5 that speaks of the blessing of the men in whose hearts are the highways to Zion. This metaphor is striking and strongly hints those who walk in the Lord's ways are on the highways to Zion in their hearts. On the level of a spiritual analogy this implies that walking in God's ways leads them to the Lord. But, it may also be a reference to those who were familiar with Psalm 84 and the Pilgrimage Psalms and who were not able to go to Jerusalem, but who journeyed there in the imagination of their hearts.

Travel for the pilgrims involved an element of danger although they would have travelled in groups and not alone. Those on their pilgrimage were strengthened by the Lord on the arduous and strenuous journey towards Jerusalem, through the valley of Baca (a place of tears or weeping) so named as it had a dangerous reputation. Because the Lord was with them they became stronger on their journey and the dry inhospitable valley of Baca was transformed into a place of springs providing refreshment. The pilgrims are on their way to meet God. But the Lord has already gone before them transforming the way, protecting them and making provision for them.

8-12   O Lord God of hosts, hear my prayer: give ear, O God of Jacob! Behold our shield O God: look upon the face of your anointed! For a day in your courts is better than a thousand elsewhere. I would rather be a doorkeeper in the house of my God than dwell in the tents of wickedness. For the Lord God is a sun and shield: he bestows favour and honour. No good thing does the Lord withhold from those who walk uprightly. O Lord of hosts, blessed is the man who trusts in you!

It would be natural for the pilgrims in the Temple to make requests in prayer. As they were likely to be there during a major festival it is natural to pray for God's blessing on the king whom they refer to as your anointed one. 'O Lord God of hosts' is used four times in Psalm 84 and this title is associated with the ark in the Holy of Holies.

This was the symbol of the Lord's presence with his people. And addressing the Lord by this title would bring to mind God as a warrior and his power in establishing his kingdom. During the festival in Jerusalem the title 'Lord of hosts' in the context of praying for the king and the nation brought to their consciousness and imagination of faith, the Lord's authority, power and rule in the life of the nation. For the pilgrim the 'Lord of hosts' represented God's presence in the Temple in Jerusalem and invoked a powerful image to be used with confidence in prayer.

In prayer seeking the blessing of 'the Lord of hosts' on the king is asking for protection from the nation's enemies and for peace. A peace that was essential for pilgrims to come to Jerusalem and spend precious time in God's presence in worship. 'Yet Yahweh's gift of favour and honour and the good things of life is not confined to the area within sight of the Temple. Its application is moral and religious not geographical. It applies to people who walk with integrity and to people who trust Yahweh wherever they live. In the absence of that walk and trust living within sight of the Temple does one no good. Conversely, the walk and trust having that effect is not open only to people who live in Jerusalem, as if Yahweh could only operate within shouting distance of the Temple.'[8]

PSALM 116

I LOVE THE LORD

Psalm 116 forms part of the Egyptian Hallel group of psalms. It is a festival psalm for corporate worship that was used at the major event of the Passover and would have been one of The Psalms sung by Jesus and his disciples. 'The psalm itself speaks of a much larger gathering in the courts of the house of the Lord in v 18-19. A major event of the kind would have been the Passover of 516 BC the first in the newly rebuilt Temple.

That in turn would have recalled the still greater assembly in the days of Josiah - 2 Chron. 35: 19.'[1]

In The Psalms the author's love for the Lord is often expressed when he testifies to God's goodness. Or when he offers thanksgiving or a sacrifice of praise. Or when he makes a vow all in the context of corporate worship. 'I love the Lord' acts as a theme that defines the whole of Psalm 116. Love calls on the name of the Lord as a lover calls out to his beloved by name and implies a bond of belonging. In v 7 the lover finds rests in the beloved who is the Lord and in v 9 the lover lives in the presence of the Lord. In v 14 and 18, the lover fulfils his vows to the beloved - the Lord and in v 16 the love of the psalmist declares to the Lord 'I am your servant.'[2]

1-4   I love the Lord, because he has heard my voice and my supplications. Because he inclined his ear to me, therefore I will call on him as long as I live. The snares of death encompassed me: the pangs of Sheol laid hold on me: I suffered distress and anguish. Then I called on the name of the Lord: O Lord, I beseech you, save my life!'

Psalm 116 is a song of thanksgiving for answered prayer for salvation by an individual in the context of corporate worship. In the Temple courts services were held in which individuals had the opportunity to bring thank offerings and to accompany their sacrificial worship with words of testimony and praise for answered prayer.[3] 'The text of the psalm required an occasion when a cup and sacrifice figured in the rituals of celebration. It found two closely connected occasions. The first was the celebration of the Passover. Psalm 116 is the fourth of the sequence of 'the Egyptian Hallel' that were read during the course of the Passover meal…The second occasion was the Lord's Supper. In the development of Christian liturgical practice Psalm 116 came to be used in the celebration of the

Eucharist, in particular and always as the psalm connected with Communion observed on Holy Thursday.'[4]

A surprising feature about Psalm 116 that is almost unique is that along with Psalm 18 they are the only two psalms that begin with the words: 'I love the Lord.' Just as there is an underlying intimacy with the Lord in The Psalms so too there is often a love for the Lord that permeates them. But, in Psalm 116, it is the Lord's love through answered prayer that prompts the psalmist to declare his love in return for the Lord. This is reminiscent of 1 John 4: 19: 'We love the Lord because he first loved us.' In v 3-4 we learn that the psalmist's life was in grave danger and that he was close to death and in desperation he called on the name of the Lord to save him. The psalmist would have associated the name of the Lord with his acts of salvation on behalf of his people Israel and would have been hoping that the Lord would also save him: and the Lord did indeed hear and save him. Clearly, the psalmist's heart is now full and overflowing with gratitude and love for the Lord that he expresses in v 1-2: 'I love the Lord - therefore I will call on him as long as I live.'

As I thought about the psalmist calling on the 'name of the Lord' and personally declaring 'I love the Lord' in Psalm 116 - my mind focused on contemporary sung worship that often does not address the Lord by name. Instead, the lyrics of many songs simply use the word 'you' throughout when speaking about Christ, God or the Lord. On the one hand the worshipper knows that 'you' refers to God or Christ. But, at the same time many of these songs could be addressed to anyone. As you look through The Psalms it is clear that the name God or Lord is used throughout in every single one of them. Also in just over 20 psalms (as in Psalm 116) the 'name of the Lord' is referred to.

The Psalms challenge us to think about the significance of addressing God personally by name as opposed to calling him 'you' - that is the tendency in contemporary worship songs. By addressing the 'Lord' or 'God' or 'Christ' or calling on the 'name of the Lord' - we are specifically identifying who we are speaking to. The name God or Lord in The Psalms speak about who God is. He is the God of Abraham, Isaac and Jacob. The God who saved the Hebrews and established Israel as his people. He is also the God and Father of our Lord Jesus Christ. So to use the name God, Christ or Lord specifically reminds us of their character and what they have done for us. It is also a sign of reverence and reminds us of their authority in heaven and earth and their salvation in our lives.

When we use the names of God, Christ and Lord they remind us of their character. Just as you would never refer to someone you were talking to as 'you' as this would be extremely rude and a derogatory term, so too The Psalms question contemporary practice that refers to God and Christ as 'you.' In the Scriptures God and Christ have innumerable names that portray their character and are more appropriate to use. On those occasions when we are introduced to someone for the first time we might comment on how beautiful or lovely their name sounds and we may well ask them what it means. So too the names of God, Christ and Lord and all the other names in Scripture that refer to them, have a beauty about them because of their meaning and significance. It is clearly time we stopped using the colloquial 'you' for God and Christ.

5-11   Gracious is the Lord and righteous: our God is merciful. The Lord preserves the simple: when I was brought low he saved me. Return O my soul to your rest: for the Lord has dealt bountifully with you. For you have delivered my soul from death,my eyes from tears, my feet from stumbling:

I walk before the Lord in the land of the living. I kept my faith even when I said, 'I am greatly afflicted.' I said in my consternation, 'Men are all a vain hope.'

Although we do not know what situation the psalmist refers to we clearly get the impression that his life was in serious danger and that death was a distinct possibility. These verses describe his considerable suffering and he was particularly concerned because humanly speaking no one had been able to help him. In v 3 he has spoken about the 'snares of death' and in v 8 he says 'you have delivered my soul from death.' Quite possibly then he is describing a potentially life threatening illness when he speaks in v 3 of being in distress and anguish and in v 8 speaks of no longer being tearful or stumbling as he walks. It is no surprise then that in v 5 he declares that the Lord has been merciful to him and very gracious in healing him. That he says in v 6 'the Lord preserves the simple' may indicate that he was not an important person like the king, so that God might look more favourably on him. In v 10 he shares how he did not lose his faith even when death seemed imminent. His trust in the Lord remained firm and he joyfully declares in v 9, 'I walk before the Lord in the land of the living!'

12-19   What shall I render to the Lord for all his bounty to me? I will lift up the cup of salvation and call on the name of the Lord, I will pay my vows to the Lord in the presence of all his people. Precious in the sight of the Lord is the death of his saints. O Lord, I am your servant, the son of your handmaid. You have loosed my bonds. I will offer to you the sacrifice of thanksgiving and call on the name of the Lord. I will pay my vows to the Lord in the presence of all his people. In the courts of the house of the Lord, in your midst, O Jerusalem. Praise the Lord!

Clearly, the psalmist's relief and gratitude to the Lord at being healed and saved from the prospect of death is immense. In v 7 'Return O my soul to your rest' sums up the transformation in his heart and mind. And what a transformation it is - for his soul is now at peace in a permanent way as God has been so good to him. Verse 12 indicates the psalmist has thought at length about how to express his gratitude to the Lord and he has concluded that it is appropriate to publicly testify to God's goodness in the Temple precincts in worship at the Passover. In this festival during the meal there were four cups of blessing and one of these was the cup of salvation. This would have provided a timely occasion for him to share his testimony of healing.

To call on the name of the Lord was also another way of witnessing to the Lord's salvation in his life. The last way of showing his gratitude was by fulfilling the vows he made while he was ill. Lifting up the cup of salvation and calling on the name of the Lord were likely to have been two of his vows. And v 16 indicates the third of these vows was to serve the Lord in some way in the courts of the Temple in Jerusalem. So great was the crisis of being so close to death for the psalmist and so great is his gratitude, love and thanksgiving to the Lord in return, that he repeats himself in v 17-19. His faith and love have been strengthened by the Lord's salvation and he publicly renews his commitment to the Lord through the vows he made and fulfilled in corporate worship.

PSALM 119

BIBLICAL INTIMACY

The model of *'biblical intimacy'* with the Lord is far, far richer, more comprehensive and imaginative than the model of *'romantic intimacy'* that is prevalent in sung worship. This is clearly seen in Psalm 119 as this is the model par excellence of *'biblical intimacy.'* This complex psalm embraces a number of themes and Brueggemann calls this 'a massive intellectual achievement.'[1] It is then somewhat surprising to find that Biblical commentators do not tend to devote a great deal of space to it even though it is the longest psalm with 176 verses. That is apart from J. M. Boice with 100 pages and J. Goldingay 2008 with 67 pages. But, they do tell us that this is an acrostic psalm. This means that for each letter of the Hebrew alphabet there is a stanza of eight verses that implies it is carefully constructed.

'Psalm 119 is structured with delicate sophistication about the life of the Spirit. On the one hand, the psalm understands that life with Yahweh is a two-way-street. Torah-Law keepers have a right to expect something from Yahweh. Obedience gives entry to seek God's attention and God's gift...This is the speech of one who has access not because of arrogance, but because of submission. The speech is not unduly deferential and certainly not strident. It is an articulation of legitimate expectation between partners who have learned to trust each other.'[2] Of all the commentators I looked at not one suggested who the author of this complex psalm might be. However, I am inclined to think that it is David for a number of reasons. The intimate knowledge of the Lord and the relationship with him the author of Psalm 119 describes and aspires to is reminiscent of David. Only a man who was anointed with the Holy Spirit and who had known the Lord closely could have composed a psalm that is resplendent with such emotional intensity. In this psalm David openly shares his love for Lord and his delight in his ways.

1-8   Blessed are those whose way is blameless who walk in the law of the Lord. Blessed are those who keep his testimonies who seek him with their whole heart, who also do no wrong, but walk in his ways! You have commanded your precepts to be kept diligently. O that my ways may be steadfast in keeping your statutes! Then I shall not be put to shame, having my eyes fixed on all your commandments. I will praise you with an upright heart, when I learn your righteous ordinances. I will observe your statutes. O forsake me not utterly!

We can perceive that the Holy Spirit inspired David to write this psalm although we do not know the background that led to it. We can sum up the essence of this psalm by saying it is about David's love for the Lord and also about his delight in his laws and Word. The psalm describes a single-minded determination to keep God's laws. It seems as if the writer is obsessed with God's commandments, his laws, his ordinances, his precepts, his statutes, his truth and his Word. But, his passionate concern is not at all a legalistic one. At the heart of Psalm 119 is David's delight in the Lord and his love for him. Although the Holy Spirit inspired him to write about these things it is the Lord who drew David into an intimate relationship with himself.

To delight in the Lord and in our intimate relationship with him invariably results in delighting in his laws and Word. The converse is also true. For David to delight in keeping God's laws and Word is a reflection of his delight in the Lord. The Law was a gift from God and it led him to the Lord: and he knew that his closeness with the Lord depended on keeping his commandments. The Spirit inspired David to write this psalm to show us the closeness we can also aspire to in our relationship with the Lord. An intimacy the Lord desires us to have with him as we learn to delight in him and his Word. As we read Psalm 119 we can perceive in David evidence of an artistic, creative and sensitive temperament. At the same time we discern a tenderness towards the Lord. In v 4 he says, 'In the way of your testimonies I delight as much as in all riches.' In v 10 he says, 'with my whole heart I seek you.' In v 35 he says, 'Lead me in the path of your commandments for I delight in it.' And in v 57 he says, 'The Lord is my portion: I promise to keep your word.'

9-16   How can a young man keep his way pure? By guarding it according to your word. With my whole heart I seek you: let me not wander from your commandments! I have laid up your word in my heart, that I might not sin against you. Blessed be thou O Lord, teach me your statutes! With my lips I declare all the ordinances of your mouth. In the way of your testimonies I delight as much as in all riches. I will meditate on your precepts, and fix my eyes on your ways. I will delight in your statutes:I will not forget your word.

To experience this passionate '*biblical intimacy*' with the Lord clearly demands a wholehearted commitment to love the Lord and to keep his Word. It also demands diligence to live in submission to the Lord and to his Word. In v 10 David sums up the desire the Lord put into his heart through the inspiration of the Holy Spirit - 'With my whole heart I seek you, let me not wander from your commandments.' The first sixteen verses of Psalm 119 give an indication of the tenacity required 'to walk in the law of the Lord,' in response to the promptings of the Spirit. The tenacity described in these verses is portrayed by David's actions: 'to walk in the law'- 'to keep his testimonies' - 'to seek him' - 'to diligently keep' - 'to steadfastly keep' - 'to be fixed on' - 'to learn' - 'to observe' - 'to guard' - 'to not wander' - 'to lay up your word' - 'to declare' - 'to delight and to meditate.'

Verses 9-16 also provide us with indispensable insights about maintaining our intimacy with the Lord. Verse 9 hints at living a pure lifestyle by based on God's Word. Verse 10 reminds us of the need to be wholehearted in our love for the Lord if we wish to enjoy a closeness with him and this is shown by keeping his commandments. Verse 11 echoes the importance of a heart that is saturated with God's Word to avoid sin. Verses 14 and 16 are an exhortation to delight in the Lord's Word and his laws and his ways. Because as we know this is an expression of our delight in the Lord himself. What Psalm 119: 1-16 does so wonderfully well is to show us that our intimacy with the Lord is not just a matter of emotion - and telling the Lord we love him and want an intimacy with him and expressing our feelings. *'Biblical intimacy'* with the Lord is firmly rooted in living an obedient life and keeping his commandments. This is a challenge to our songwriters to write songs about our love and intimacy with the Lord that express the ways in which we can keep his Word and his commandments.

The Lord calls us to be in a close relationship with him and have an intimate walk with him but it does not come easily. What is demanded is similar to the desire required to acquire wisdom in Proverbs 2: 1-10. In these verses the author points out to the young man that to gain wisdom is demanding and a very strenuous task. To achieve this in v 2 he has to be attentive to wisdom and incline his heart to understanding. In v. 3 he has to cry out for insight and raise his voice for understanding. In v 4 he has to seek it like silver and search for it as for hidden treasure. Verse 5 indicates that only then will he understand the fear of the Lord and find the knowledge of God. Verse 6 informs us that it is the Lord who gives wisdom and from his mouth come knowledge and understanding. On the one hand they are gifts of God's grace. But, these verses also imply the Lord will only give these things to the person who wholeheartedly longs for and diligently seeks them.

Having read the opening verses of Psalm 119: 1-16 one might be led to believe that David enjoyed a carefree life without any difficulties or troubles and one full of God's blessings. But, as this psalm progresses this is clearly not true. Interspersed throughout is the allusion to his enemies and their persecution. This theme is representative of many of David's psalms and strongly indicates he is the author of Psalm 119. We see evidence of his enemies in the following verses: 21-23, 42, 51, 61, 69, 78, 84-87, 95, 98, 110, 121, 157 and 161. What is striking about these verses is that while they refer to David's persecution in every instance he declares his commitment and faithfulness to the Lord. The following verses describe the impact of his enemies upon him. He says in v 15 'they utterly deride me' - v 22 'their scorn and contempt of me' - v 42 'those who taunt me' - v 69 'they besmear me' - v 78 'they subvert me' - v 110 'a snare has been laid for me.' Moreover, on three occasions there comes an appeal for life in the midst of danger as in verses 169-176. Unsurprisingly, prayer for deliverance is linked to these occasions. We first get a glimpse of David's prayer interspersed in this psalm in v 25, 'My soul cleaves to the dust: revive me according to your word.' His prayer is repeated in verses 88, 134 and in v 173 - 'Let your hand be ready to help me, for I have chosen your precepts.'

For David who on occasions was involved in battles against Israel's enemies and against Saul their opposition during his life was a cause of concern for him. His enemies were the reality he faced alongside that of knowing the Lord intimately. His faith and love for the Lord was refined and tested in the circumstantial events he was caught up in. Yet, he believed that the Lord was involved in his life and caught up in protecting and rescuing him from his enemies. Rather than turn him away from the Lord persecution taught him to rely on the Lord and trust him to save him. *(Although on occasions he failed to turn to the Lord for help as in 1 Sam. 27 when he turned to Achish and stayed in the land of the Philistines).* One of the themes that is interwoven into Psalm 119 alongside that of his enemies and the danger they pose to his life and future, is the theme of 'promise.' This is recorded in verses: 38, 41, 49-50, 58, 76, 82, 116, 123, 133 and 140.

There are two different types of promise that David is referring to. The first is a conditional promise that means that God will bless those who keep his laws as stated in Exodus. Failure to keep God's laws means you forfeit the promised blessing. A conditional promise is one that David refers to at the beginning of Psalm 119: 1-2. 'Blessed are those whose way is blameless, who walk in the law of the Lord. Blessed are those who keep his testimonies, who seek him with their whole heart.' This blessing is in keeping with God's promises in Exodus. It is also a promise of knowing God's steadfast love and faithfulness. Having his life threatened by his enemies along with the risk of being killed by them is seen by David as a violation of this blessing, so he claims the promise of deliverance, protection and salvation. But, there is also another very important promise that David alludes to as he considers the possible threat to his life. This is an unconditional promise from the Lord and does not depend at all on him keeping God's laws. In effect God has promised to bless David regardless of his obedience or failure. This unconditional promise can be found in Psalm 89: 3-4 and in 2 Samuel 7: 8-29.

Psalm 89: 3-4:
I have made a covenant with my chosen one
I have sworn to my servant David:
I will establish your descendents for ever
and build your throne for all generations.

2 Samuel 7: 11-16:
Moreover the Lord declares to you that the Lord
will make you a house. When your days are
fulfilled and you lie down with your fathers I will
raise up your offspring after you, who shall come
forth from your body and I will establish his
kingdom. He shall build a house for my name *and*
I will establish the throne of his kingdom forever. I
will be his father and he shall be my son. When he

commits iniquity I will chasten him with the rod of men, with the stripes of the sons of men: but I will not take my steadfast love from him as I took it from Saul whom I put away before you. *And your house and your kingdom shall be made sure for ever before me: your throne shall be established for ever.*

Even in the context of his intimate walk with the Lord and the demands this makes on David he tenaciously reminds God of his promise and in prayer asks him to fulfill it. Bearing in mind David's experience of the Lord and the declaration of his love for him and his delight in his ways, it does seem an extraordinary failure by him that led to his sin with Bathsheba which in turn resulted in God's punishment upon his own family. But, despite this, God kept his promise to David and Solomon inherited the kingdom, although later in his life it was divided due to his sin with his concubines and foreign wives. As David was a direct ancestor of Christ God fulfilled his promise to him about having a direct descendent on his throne.

The other prayer David offered to the Lord was for help to keep his commandments and to love him. This is seen in v 10, 'With my whole heart I seek you, let me not wander from your commandments.' Verses 32-36 are also a good example of this.

I will run in the way of your commandments when you enlarge my understanding. Teach me O Lord the way of your statutes and I will keep it to the end. Give me understanding that I may keep your law and observe it with my whole heart. Lead me in the path of your commandments for I delight in it. Incline my heart to your testimonies and not to gain.

Psalm 119 epitomises what *'biblical intimacy'* with the Lord is at its best. It represents the Lord's desire for us to have a intimate walk with him. It also symbolises the reality of our lives alongside our own difficulties and trials. It presents us with the challenge to nurture a tender relationship with the Lord. And it also reminds us that we prayerfully need his help to fulfill the potential of *'biblical intimacy'* with the Lord.

PSALM 139

INSIDE OUT!

As I was worshipping the Lord through Holy Communion on my own one morning in 2009, the Lord reminded me that he has known me intimately since I was a very young teenager and that he also knows and understands me better than anyone else. This inspired me to write my first book on 'The Psalms - Intimacy, Doxology & Theology' - 2010. Biblical commentators say Psalm 139 is to be used in corporate worship as it contains magnificent truths about God. This psalm is important in the context of worship as it shows how the Lord knows each one of us intimately and personally. He knows us inside out. It can also readily be recognised as a devotional classic and one in which Christians are often likely to use the first eight verses in isolation from 19-24, to give a sense of assurance that the Lord knows all about us and that his hand is on our lives. From this perspective it is an encouraging sign of the Lord's love as he knows each of us perfectly. He knows all our funny little ways, our quirks and the different facets of our personality. He knows what makes each one of us tick. He understands us completely and also what   to others are the contradictory aspects of our personality. We may even perceive that the Lord is like a counsellor or psychologist with whom we can share our innermost thoughts and feelings.

The truths about the Lord in Psalm 139 are in the context of the testing and the obedience of the psalmist. For those who are disobedient this psalm presents a considerable challenge as it reminds them they cannot hide anything from the Lord. Therefore, the truths about the Lord in this psalm are likely to make them feel uncomfortable and convict them. For those who are walking in the Lord's ways this psalm is reassuring as when they are tested by the Lord they can be confident of his hand upon their lives. It is also a reminder there are occasions in our lives when the Lord allows our faith to be tested. We see this in the lives of Abraham, David and Job, whose testing took place over a prolonged period. We also see it in Jesus' life when he was led by the Holy Spirit to be tested by the Devil in the wilderness. Even though the Lord knows us intimately this does not exclude testing us.

Psalm 139 can also be seen as an invasion of our privacy that some may find disconcerting. After all, what is there to hide from God that he doesn't already know? And at times there may well be things that we deliberately hold back from the Lord or may subconsciously hide from him. J. Goldingay points out that in his classes on The Psalms there are students who see this psalm as good news and those who see it as bad news and those who more perceptively discern that its interpretation depends on who you are![1]

We have no precise details from this psalm to know what the circumstances were in David's life that led to its composition. While some commentators think there is an air of ambiguity about how the psalmist responded to the truths about the Lord, the issue is whether David is secure in the knowledge that the Lord knows all there is to know about him. Or, if he is somewhat fearful and hesitant in case any hidden sinful traits are discovered by the Lord. I am inclined to think the internal evidence of this psalm answers this in a positive manner and that David was not at all apprehensive of being tested by the Lord. Moreover, as he doesn't allude to or mention any specific sin that has been discovered in his life through God's searching and testing we can conclude that none was found.

While we may initially perceive that the insights in this psalm are David's v 17 hints that these initially originate from the Lord himself. This is evident when he says, 'How precious to me are your thoughts O God!' We can assume that at one particular point in time the Lord thought it was appropriate to reassure him that his hand was on his life: and that he was with him constantly and that he understood him completely and knew him intimately. This would have filled David with confidence and removed any doubts that he may have had about the future. Presumably, as the Lord considered it important to speak to him about the truths contained in this psalm we may speculate that David had been troubled about these things. One possibility is that this reflects the period in his life when he was pursued by Saul and his men who sought to kill him. As he was on the run for quite some time before he was crowned king question marks about his future probably surfaced in his mind. Quite, possibly then, the Lord graciously revealed the truths in this psalm to reassure David and boost his confidence and faith in the Lord and reassure him about His future plans for him.

1-6   O Lord you have searched me and known me!
           You know when I sit down and when I rise
           up: you discern my thoughts from afar. You
           search out my path and my lying down and
           are acquainted with all my ways. Even before a
           word is on my tongue, lo O Lord you know it
           altogether. You go behind me and before me
           and lay your hand upon me. Such knowledge is
           too wonderful for me: it is high I cannot attain it.

Although the Lord took the initiative that led to the inspiration of this psalm it is not a sentimental one. The Lord revealed to David that not only was his hand on his life and that he knew him intimately but that for some time now he had been testing him. That he is acutely aware of this is seen by the way he begins this psalm in v 1: 'O Lord you have searched me and known me!' The

Hebrew word for 'search' means to 'dig' - as in searching for some precious metal - other Biblical commentators see the interpretation as winnowing or sifting that indicates refining. The Lord had been looking into David's heart to test him although he already knew all there was to know about him. He didn't need to 'dig down' or 'search' or look into his heart and life. But, his motive in revealing his action to David is to make him aware of the fact that this is what the Lord was doing. It is not as if the Lord needed to find out anything he already wasn't aware of. But, this was a refining process in his faith the Lord wanted him to be aware of because it was beneficial to him in his relationship with the Lord.

Psalm 139 readily divides into four sections. Verses 1-6 refer to God's omniscience - God is all knowing. Verses 7-12 refer to God's omnipresence - God's divine presence and v 13-16 refer to God's omnificence - God's creative power, while v 19-24 speak about God's testing. To begin with the assertion that the Holy Spirit inspired David to write this psalm because the Lord wanted to reveal the truths its contains about Him to David - we then have to conclude that it is the Lord who is actually speaking through these verses, although initially it sounds as if these thoughts are David's. So when he speaks in v 2-5 this is actually what the Lord revealed to David. The Lord informed him that he knew all about him - completely and utterly. And it may be that this was the first time this had touched him in such a profound way because it was meaningful to him in his circumstances.

In v 6 which is David's response of awe and wonder to v 1-5 this confirms that the content of the previous verses do indeed originate with the Lord. Therefore, it is safe to assume that the entire contents of this psalm are the Lord's thoughts revealed to David. They do not originate with him but rather through them the Lord addresses in very personal terms certain questions that have arisen in David's mind. A. Weiser eloquently captures their mystical element: 'It shows the simultaneous interaction of awe and wonder at the inconceivable greatness of God and of devoted trustful submission to him. As the poet looks back over his life he sees it beneath the searching eye of God, which has always rested and still rests upon him. No matter where he may look or whether he stands still or walks, sits, or lies down, everywhere he meets the searching eye of God testing him and watching him continually: indeed God even knows what he is going to say before he has uttered a word and even discerns his thoughts from afar. These verses express the astonishment of a man who discovers that in all his ways he is involved with relations which remain hidden from the natural eye: that he no longer entirely belongs to himself or lives exclusively for his own sake, because it points every-where to those invisible bonds which unite him to the reality of God.'[2]

7-12   Where shall I flee from your Spirit? Or where shall I flee from your presence? If I ascend to heaven you are there! If I make my bed in Sheol you are there! If I take the wings of the morning and dwell in the uttermost parts the sea, even there your hand shall lead me and your right hand shall hold me. If I say 'Let only darkness cover me and the light about me be night,' even the darkness is not dark to you, the night is bright as the day: for darkness is as light with you.

The implication of v 7-12 is that when the Lord is testing David it is of no use whatsoever to try to escape from him or run away. There is nowhere in the universe where we can hide from the Lord's presence. His searching eye sees everywhere and he will find us. The Holy Spirit revealed to David's heart that when He is testing him he cannot hide from Him as the Lord can see whatever he is doing. God is in heaven. God is in the depths of the earth. God is even in the farthest parts of the ocean. No matter where he is or whatever his circumstances are the Spirit shows David that even there the Lord's hand will lead him and his right hand is upon him. In our lives we can discern that the significance of the Lord searching and testing us is because he desires to maintain a close intimate fellowship with us. If for any reason we are not walking in his ways this will affect our relationship with the Lord. The meaning and purpose of 'searching and testing' is to eliminate any sin or displeasing issues in our lives as the Lord reveals them to us in the process of being refined.

13-18   For you formed my inward parts, you did knit me together in my mother's womb. I praise you, for you are fearful and wonderful. Wonderful are your works! You know me completely: my frame was not hidden from you when I was being made in secret, intricately wrought in the depths of the earth. Your eyes beheld my unformed substance: in your book were written every one of them, the days that were formed for me, when as yet there was none of them. How precious to me are your thoughts O God! How vast is the sum of them! If I could count them, they are more than the sand. When I awake, I am still with you.

In v 2 the knowledge that the Lord has of David pales into the background in comparison to the incomparably profound knowledge of him that the Lord reveals in v 13-16. It is one thing for the Lord to be familiar with the ordinary, everyday issues of what David is doing, saying, sitting or thinking. It is quite another to reveal to David that his knowledge of him is far, far more profound than he had ever imagined or realised. When he was in his mother's womb and being formed and had no conscious awareness of the Lord - the Lord looked upon him and saw him being intricately formed - v 16: 'Your eyes beheld my unformed substance.' The Lord is clearly telling David that he knows him in a most unique way.

Moreover, the Lord impresses on his heart that not only was he present when he was in the womb he also knew the plans that he had for him in the future even before he was born. From these verses as the Lord spoke to David about his future that he had planned before his birth we can imagine him having a tremendous sense of assurance that considerably strengthened his faith. This indicates the future was an issue he had been greatly concerned about. His response in v 17, 'How precious to me are your thoughts O God!' is an appropriate one to what the Lord has revealed to David.

19-24   O that you would slay the wicked O God, and that men of blood would depart from me, men who maliciously defy you, who lift themselves up against you for evil. Do I not hate them that hate you O Lord? And do I not loathe them that rise up against you? I hate them with perfect hatred: I count them my enemies. Search me, O God and know my heart! Try me and know my thoughts! And see if there be any wicked way in me, and lead me in the way everlasting!

The introduction of the wicked in v 19-22 appears problematic and out of place with what has gone before. If we assume the Lord tested David and spoke to reassure him about his future in v 19 the wicked and the men of blood can possibly be seen as his enemies who might affect his future. Indeed, they might even have occasion to kill him. J. Mays comments: 'The vehement sentiments seem so inconsistent that some have suggested they are a crude addition, and so unacceptable to religious sensibility that they are customarily omitted in liturgical and theological use. But, in the thought world of The Psalms this section is not at all incoherent...In the worldview of The Psalms the wicked and their dangerous threats to those who base life on God are an important part of the reality in the midst of which faith must live.

It is probably a mistake to take v 19 as a real petition directed against some particular identifiable threat. The style of the wish is rather to be read as a form of the description of the self in relationship with God.'[3] In the language and world view of his day David is in effect saying, 'I will walk in the paths of righteousness rather than in the way of the wicked.' Therefore, he affirms his allegiance to the Lord which is in striking contrast to the wicked who are God's enemies and do not walk in his ways. This dovetails with v 23-24 when David himself invites the Lord at the end of this psalm: 'Search me O God and know my heart! Try me and know my thoughts! And see if there be any wicked way in me, and lead me in the way everlasting!' He denounces the wicked and their ways and invites the Lord to search him and reveal any wicked way in his life that is displeasing to the Lord that he might repent of it.

David also acknowledges two important things. Firstly, as the Lord searches his heart there may be sin in his life that is displeasing to him that he is unaware of or which he is turning a blind eye to. Secondly, he asks the Lord for his help to walk in his ways. This searching, examining activity of the Lord in our lives reminds me of Cranmer's Collect For Purity. Because it also invites the Lord to search our hearts by his Spirit to reveal any hidden sins, alongside the exhortation to love the Lord and to ask for his help to do so.

> Almighty God
> To whom all hearts are open
> All desires known
> And from whom no secrets are hidden:
> Cleanse the thought of our hearts
> By the inspiration of your Holy Spirit
> That we may perfectly love you
> And worthily magnify your holy name:
> Through Jesus Christ our Lord - Amen.

PSALM 145

I EXTOL YOU

In Psalms 145-150 there is immediately an uplifting atmosphere of worship. Psalm 145 is David's last psalm and while in many of them he expresses his feelings and looks for help in this he objectively and exclusively focuses on the Lord. It is also a prophetic psalm as inspired by the Holy Spirit he anticipates that the Lord will be praised throughout history. Looking back in the 21st century his prediction rings true. From a literal perspective there is not only an abundance but also a superabundance of reasons in this psalm about how and why we should praise the Lord which could have conceivably ended at v 13 followed by v 21. My instinctive reaction to this ambitious psalm of praise is that it should be regularly used in corporate worship, because it speaks of God's greatness, goodness and provision: and it also speaks about the Lord as King and his kingdom and people throughout history praising the Lord.

1-3   I will extol you my God and King, and bless your name for ever and ever. Every day I will bless you, and praise your name for ever and ever. Great is the Lord and greatly to be praised and his greatness is unsearchable.

J. M. Boice calls this a 'monumental praise psalm.'[1] Clearly, there is considerable justification for this as it contains superlative praise that is predicted to be unending. David declares in v 1: 'Every day I will bless you' and this gives us a template that acts as a model of praise. This increases progressively throughout the psalm as others join in. In this psalm David echoes his lifelong commitment to praise the Lord and to worship him. Verse 1 echoes how personal an expression this is when he says: 'I will extol you, My God and king.' This is not a poem in praise of an unknown god. It is offered to the Lord, the

Creator, who has a personal relationship with David. As he offers his praise to the Lord he focuses on the twin aspects of God's character - his greatness and his goodness. What stands out in The Psalms and speaks to us is the intuitive sense of how appropriate it is for individuals, the community and the nations to praise the Lord and worship him. Just as we instinctively look to voice our admiration by praising an accomplished artist of a particular skill, so too David's heart is full of worship for the Lord which he cannot silently contain as his heart is bursting with praise.

Praise is complete when it is offered and received. Not to speak out and remain silent and refuse to praise when it is deserved is tantamount to sin. But, in contrast, there is a joyful liberty when we offer praise to the Lord, our Creator, that is clearly his due. Yet, we should take care not to overlook that David the king is extolling the Lord as his King and praising his name. In Isaiah 43: 15 we read: I am the Lord, your Holy One, the Creator of Israel, your King.' Hence in v 3 there is the appropriate acclamation, 'Great is the Lord, and greatly to be praised, and his greatness is unsearchable.' There is no end to it. It cannot be fathomed. It goes on forever. The Lord as King speaks of his authority, his power and his rule over all earthly rulers and nations.

4-7   One generation shall declare your works to an-
       other and shall declare your mighty acts. On
       the glorious splendour of your majesty, and on
       your wondrous works I will meditate. Men shall
       proclaim your mighty acts and I will declare your
       greatness. They shall pour forth the fame of your
       abundant goodness and shall sing aloud of your
       righteousness.

In v 1-3 David begins to praise the Lord and in v 4 predicts one generation after another shall praise the Lord. In v 5 David praises the Lord and in v 6 men praise the

Lord. In v. 8-9 David praises the Lord and in v 10 all the works of the Lord and all of God's saints shall praise the Lord. In v 13-20 David focuses on the Lord's character and in v 21 he praises the Lord. Also in v 21, the last verse, everyone shall praise the Lord and bless his holy name for ever and ever. The climax builds to a crescendo of praise to which there is no foreseeable end. M. Wilcock sees this psalm as a *'tour de force'* and says, 'We cannot fail to be struck by the psalmist's artistic skill, his breadth of vision and the deceptive simplicity of his message.'[2] No doubt he means it is profound. Weiser informs us that despite its personal style it is a liturgical hymn of the cult community and it was possibly recited at the feast of the covenant and is modelled on the idea of the kingship of Yahweh which played an important part.[3]

Many modern songs focus on the believer's feelings and can make themselves the object of their worship but here in these six psalms 145-150 we cannot help but get lost in the wonder, love and praise of the Lord. Here God is the object and subject of our praise and worship and it is liberating when we take delight in expressing our praise and worship to the Lord. In Psalm 145 there is an almost seamless move between God's greatness and goodness and the inference is that you cannot separate the two as the latter is an expression of the former. David's worship is clearly bound up with these twin themes.[4]

The flow of Psalm 145 is marked by the repetition of themes. As we have seen praising the Lord begins with David as an individual, moves to generation after generation, to men, to all the works of the Lord, to all the saints and then to where everyone praises the Lord for ever and ever. This is a symphony of praise that extols God's greatness and goodness throughout history. This psalm alternates between declarations of praise and God's character, his greatness or goodness. Intermingled in the psalm is also an element of testifying or witnessing to these attributes of the Lord. The Christian community at praise is one that testifies to what the Lord has done for them and acts as a witness to others. I wonder if we are too slow in our corporate worship to testify to God's goodness? I would say we are. Yet, on the rare occasions when Christians do share what the Lord has done in their lives this is a powerful testimony. Perhaps, then our evangelistic services should include less preaching and more testimony!

Psalm 145 is also a testimony to God's provision for all of his creation. The psalm challenges communities and nations to acknowledge and recognise that all that they have comes from the hand of the Lord. An appropriate response is for our political leaders to testify to God's goodness and call their communities and nations to praise the Lord and worship him. To do this is to acknowledge God's kingdom and his rule and reign in our lives. A considerable challenge to the political structures of our day but it is not without precedent. Verses 12-13 speak of 'the glorious splendour of your kingdom. Your kingdom is an everlasting kingdom and your dominion endures throughout all generations.' J. Mays points out that it is interesting to find there is an Aramaic version of these references to God's kingdom that turn up in Daniel 4: 3 and 4: 34, as Nebuchadnezzar's praise of the God of heaven.[5] We may also see an allusion to God's kingdom in the Lord's prayer: 'your kingdom come and your will be done.' The reference to God's kingdom and his rule and provision in this psalm could have easily fallen into the trap of being escapist or one that didn't face the reality of the poor or oppressed. But, in v 14-20 this is not the case as the worshipping community is reminded of God's care and concern for them. On a personal level Psalm 145 also challenges Christians to submit their lives to God's reign. It encourages us to trust the Lord is sovereign and that his authority and power far exceeds that of human rulers. The throne room of heaven is where the Lord reigns and mention of his dominion, might, majesty, power and splendour reinforces these theological truths from a perspective of faith.

Brueggemann has this to say about Psalm 145, 'This psalm is rooted in Israel's oldest confession of God's fidelity. It is filled with utterly trusting participles that testify to God's enduring, utterly reliable actions...In this utterance, Israel at praise (and the Church in its wake) dares to assert that all of life is held within God's sustaining governance...The psalm is an evangelical act that invites a deep departure from the greed system of self-securing, nothing less than a redefinition of reality against our crippling ideologies.'[6]

FOOTNOTES

CHAPTER ONE

PSALM 2

1. O. E. Phillips Exploring The Messianic Psalms Hebrew Christian Fellowship 1967 15
2. P. C. Craigie Psalms 1-50 Word 1983 64-65
3. J. L. Mays Psalms John Knox 1994 49
4. P. C. Craigie ibid 68
5. Ibid 65
6. E. S. Gerstenberger Psalms Part 1 Eerdmans 1991 48
7. J. L. Mays ibid 44
8. J. L. Mays The Lord Reigns John Knox 1994 109
9. Ibid 101
10 T. Wilson The Messianic Psalms Loiseaux Brothers 1978 12
11. K. Schaefer Psalms Studies In Hebrew Narrative & Poetry Liturgical Press 2001 8
12. K. Schaefer ibid 9
13. J. L. Mays The Lord Reigns ibid 110-111
14. Ibid 113
15. E. S. Gerstenberger ibid 49
16. Ibid 46
17. J. L. Mays Psalms ibid 50
18. Ibid 50
19. J. Mays The Lord Reigns ibid 111
20. P. C. Craigie ibid 69
21. E. S Gerstenberger ibid 49
22. K. Schaefer ibid 10
23. P. C. Craigie ibid 69

PSALM 16

1. J. M. Boice Psalms Vol 1 Baker 1994 369 footnote 4
2. A. Weiser The Psalms John Knox 1962 173
3. J. L. Mays Psalms ibid 88
4. T. Wilson ibid 81
5. M. Wilcox Psalms 1-72 IVP 2001 57
6. K. Schaefer ibid 39
7. Ibid 38
8. T. Wilson ibid 88
9. P. C. Craigie ibid 158
10. M. Wilcox ibid 58

PSALM 18
1. O. E. Phillips ibid 39
2. P. C. Craigie ibid 172
3. M. Wilcock Psalms 1-72 ibid 61

PSALM 22
ABANDONED
1. A. Weiser ibid 219
2. J. Mays Preaching & Teaching The Psalms John Knox 2006 109-110,
3. J. L. Mays Psalms ibid 107
4. J. Goldingay Psalms Vol I Baker 2006 324-325
5. E. S. Gerstenberger Psalms Part 1 ibid 109-110
6. J. Magonet A Rabbi Reads The Psalms SCM 1994 102
7. J. Goldingay ibid 325-326
8. D. Tidball The Cross IVP 2003 86-87
9. Ibid 88
10. Ibid 89
11. M. Wilcox IVP 2001 84
12. K. Schaefer ibid 53
13. A. Weiser ibid 224-225
14. R. M. Kidd With One Voice Baker 2005 78

PSALM 22
THE CRUCIFIXION
1. T. Wilson ibid 59-60
2. J. Goldingay ibid 324
3. J. Mays Preaching & Teaching The Psalms ibid 105-106
4. J. M. Boice ibid 193
5. F. D. Bruner Matthew 13-28 Eerdmans 1990 747
6. Ibid 745
7. J. Moltmann The Crucified God SCM 1974 203, 205-206
8. J. Mattison The Seven Words Of Christ Augsburg 1992 41
9. D. Coggan The Voice From The Cross Triangle 1993 36, 35
10. F. D. Bruner ibid 749
11. Ibid 749-750
12. J. Goldingay ibid 330
13. T. Wilson ibid 63-64
14. K. Schaefer Psalms ibid 54
15. O. E. Phillips ibid 74
16. T. Wilson 64
17. O. E. Phillips ibid 75
18. O. E. Phillips ibid 76
19. J. M. Boice ibid 196

PSALM 24

1. B. Pickett The Psalms In Life & Liturgy DLT 2002 10-11
2. D. Kidner The Psalms Tyndale 1973 127
3. M. Wilcox ibid 89
4. P. C. Craigie ibid 214
5. J. L. Crenshaw Psalms Eerdmans 2001 156
6. J. Mays Psalms ibid 123
7. J. L. Crenshaw ibid 156
8. M. Glazier Psalms Of The Jewish Liturgy Aviv Press 2009 18
9. M. Wilcox ibid 88
10. J. M. Boice ibid 219
11. T. Wilson ibid 118
12. J. M. Boice 214-215
13. J. L. Mays Psalms ibid 122-123

PSALM 40

1. M. Wilcox Psalms 1-72 ibid 142
2. K. Schaefer ibid 101
3. T. Wilson ibid 26-27
4. P. C. Craigie ibid 317
5. J. Mays Psalms ibid 170
6. C. Spurgeon Psalms Vol 2 Crossway 1993 165

PSALM 45

1. T. Wilson ibid 106-107
2. J. M. Boice Vol 2 ibid 861 see footnote 4
3. Ibid 381
4. Ibid 383
5. J. L. Mays Psalms ibid 180
6. T. Wilson ibid 112
7. P. C. Craigie ibid 339
8. J. Limburg Psalms John Knox 2000 151
9. C. Spurgeon Psalms Vol 1 Crossway 1993 189
10 F. F. Bruce Hebrews Eerdmans 1990 339
11. J. L. Mays Psalms ibid 182
12. T. Wilson ibid 112
13. P. C. Craigie ibid 341

PSALM 68

1. A. Weiser ibid 481
2. J. Mays Psalms ibid 225
3. J. M. Boice Psalms 42-106 1996 553
4. M. E. Tate Psalms 51-100 Word 1990 185-186
5. J. M. Boice ibid 543-544
6. M. E. Tate ibid 173
7. K. Schaefer ibid 163

8. E. S. Gerstenberger Psalms Part 2 2001 37
9. A. Weiser ibid 484
10. K. Schaefer ibid 163
11. J. Goldingay Psalms Vol 2 Eerdmans 2007 324
12. T. Wilson ibid 94-95
13. O. E. Phillips ibid 145
14. O. Brien Ephesians Eerdmans 1999 290
15. Ibid 291
16. Ibid 288-289
17. Ibid 289
18. T. Wilson ibid 97-98
19. O. E. Phillips 147-148
20. J. M. Boice ibid 562-565

PSALM 69

1. T. Wilson ibid 71-72
2. J. L. Mays Psalms ibid 232
3. J. Goldingay Psalms Vol 2 ibid 338
4. A. Weiser ibid 493
5. M. Wilcox Psalms 1-72 ibid 241
6. J. Goldingay ibid 343
7. M. E. Tate ibid 196
8 E. S. Geerstenberger Psalms Part 2 ibid 49-50
9. J. L. Mays Psalms ibid 232-233
10. M. Wilcox ibid 243
11. K. Scaefer ibid 166-167
12. J. M. Boice ibid 578-580
13. K. Schaefer ibid 167
14. T. Wilson ibid 77-78

PSALM 72

1. M. E. Tate. Ibid 222
2. K. Schaefer ibid 174
3. J. Goldingay Psalms Vol 2 ibid 383
4. Ibid 384
5. A. Weiser ibid 503
6. Ibid 502
7. M. E. Tate ibid 225
8. M. Wilcox Psalms 1-72 ibid 251
9. K. Schaefer ibid 174
10. P. D. Miller Power, Justice & Peace Psalm 72
Faith & Mission 4 No 1 1986 65
11. D. Kidner Psalms 1-72 IVP 1973 254
12. K. Schaefer ibid 174
13. A. Weiser ibid 505

PSALM 110

1. E. S. Gerstenberger Psalms Part 2 ibid 264
2. J. L. Mays Psalms ibid 351
3. Ibid 350
4. J. M. Boice Psalms Vol 3 Baker 1998 892
5. L. C. Allen Psalms 101-150 Word 1983 83
6. C. Spurgeon Treasury of David Vol 2 Zondervan 1968 460
7. T. Wilson ibid 127
8. J. L. Mays Psalms ibid 350
9. T. Wilson ibid 128
10. J. Goldingay Psalms Vol 3 Baker 2008 295
11. T. Wilson ibid 131
12. O. E. Phillips ibid 276
13. C. Spurgeon Psalms Vol 2 ibid 130
14. J. M. Boice ibid 899
15. A. Weiser ibid 697
16. O. E. Phillips ibid 133
17. K. Schaefer ibid 274

PSALM 118

1. A. Weiser ibid 724
2. M. Glazer ibid 94
3. J. Mays ibid 378
4. M. Wilcock ibid 191-192
5. A. Weiser ibid 724
6. Ibid 726
7. Ibid 728
8. J. Goldingay Psalms Vol 3 ibid 362
9. J. Mays ibid 379-380
10. T. Wilson 176-177
11. Ibid 177

CHAPTER TWO

PSALM 6

1. J. L. Myas Psalms ibid 62
2. M. Glazer ibid 51-52
3. K. Schaefer ibid 17,19
4. J. L. Mays Psalms ibid
5. Ibid 60
6. W. Brueggemann The Psalms - The Life Of Faith
   Fortress Press 1995 54
7. Ibid 54
8. Ibid 54
9. Ibid 56
10. K. Schaefer ibid 18
11. W. Brueggemann ibid 102

12. J. M. Boice Psalms Vol 1 ibid 55
13. J. Goldingay Psalms Vol 1 ibid 137
14. P. C. Craigie ibid 93
15. J. Goldingay ibid 139
16. K. Schaefer 18
17. Ibid 19
18. Ibid 19

PSALM 18

1. P. C. Craigie ibid 172
2. J. Goldingay Psalms Vol 1 ibid 254-255
3. M. Wilcock Psalms 1-72 ibid 61
4. P. C. Craigie ibid 173
5. M. Wilcock Psalms 1-72 ibid 61
6. J. Goldingay Psalms Vol 1 ibid 257
7. M. Wilcock ibid 62
8. P. C. Craigie Ibid 173
9. A. Wesier ibid 190
10. Ibid 189

PSALM 23

1. J. Mays Psalms ibid 116-117
2. P. C. Craigie ibid 205-206
3. J, Mays Psalms ibid 119
4. M. Wilcock ibid 86
5. J. M. Boice Vol 1 ibid 211
6. A. Weiser ibid 231

PSALM 37

1. K. Schaefer ibid 92
2. J. Goldingay Psalms Vol 2 ibid 518
3. R. Van Harn & B. Strawn Editors Psalms In Preaching & Worship Eerdmans 2009 145
4. J. L. Mays Psalms ibid 160
5. K. Schaefer ibid 92
6. J. Goldingay Psalms Vol 1 ibid 519
7. S. Christou The Psalms, Intimacy, Doxology & Theology Phoenix Books 2009 85
8. A. Weiser ibid 318
9. Ibid 318
10. W. Brueggemann The Psalms ibid 249
11. Ibid 237

PSALM 42

1. M. Wilcocks ibid 151-152
2. J. Mays ibid 174
3. P. C. Craigie ibid 326
4. J. Goldingay Vol 2 ibid 27

5. Ibid 27
6. P. C. Craigie ibid 327

PSALM 43

1. Ibid 328
2. J. Goldingay Vol 2 ibid 30-31
3. A. Weiser ibid 351
4. Ibid 352

PSALM 63

1. J. M. Boice Psalms Vol 2 42-106 Baker 1996 517
2. J. Goldingay Vol 2 ibid 255
3. A. Weiser ibid 454-455
4. M. E. Tate ibid 129

PSALM 84

1. C. C. Broyles Psalms Hendrickson 1999 261
2. M. Wilcock ibid 47
3. J. Mays ibid 274
4. J. Goldingay Vol 2 ibid 588
5. J. M. Boice Vol 2 ibid 688-689
6. A. Weiser ibid 566
7. J. Goldingay ibid 589
8. A. Weiser ibid 566
9. J. Goldingay ibid 601-102

PSALM 116

1. M. Wilcock Psalms 73-150 ibid 184
2. J, Mays Psalms ibid 370-371
3. L. C. Allen Psalms 101-150 Word 1983 115
4. J. Mays ibid 371-372

PSALM 119

1. W. Brueggemann The Message Of The Psalms ibid 39
2. Ibid 41

PSALM 139

1. J. Goldingay Vol 2 ibid 640
2. A. Weiser ibid 802-803
3. J. Mays Psalms ibid 428

PSALM 145

1. J. M. Boice Psalms Vol 3 ibid 1250
2. M. Wilcock ibid 271
3. A. Weiser ibid 826-827
4. J. Goldingay Psalms Baker 1998 Vol 3 ibid 961
5. J. Mays Psalm ibid 438-439
6. W. Brueggemann The Psalms ibid 124

BIBLIOGRAPHY

L. C. Allen Psalms 101-150 Word 1983

J. M. Boice Psalms 1-41 Baker 1994

J. M. Boice Psalms 42-106 Baker 1996

J. M. Boice Psalms 107-150 Baker 1998

C. G. Broyles Psalms Hendrickson Publishers 1999

F. F. Bruce Hebrews Eerdmans 1990

W. Brueggemann The Psalms & The Life Of Faith Fortress 1995

F. D. Bruner Matthew 13-28 Eerdmans 1990

S. Christou The Psalms Phoenix Books 2010

J. L. Crenshaw The Psalms Eerdmans 2001

D. Coggan The Voice From The Cross Triangle 1993

C. A. Craigie Psalms 1-50 Word 1983

E. S. Gerstenberger Psalms Part 1 Eerdmans 1991

E. S. Gerstenberger Psalms Part 2 Eerdmans 2001

J. Goldingay Psalms Vol 1 1-41 Baker 2006

J. Goldingay Psalms Vol 2 42-89 Baker 2007

J. Goldingay Psalms Vol 3 90-150 Baker 2008

M . Glazer Psalms Of The Jewish Liturgy AVIV Press 2009

R. M. Kidd With One Voice Baker 2005

D. Kidner The Psalms Tyndale 1973

J. Limburg Psalms John Knox 2000

J. Magonet A Rabbi Reads The Psalms SCM 1998

J. Mattison The Seven Words Of Christ Augsburg 1992

J. L. Mays Psalms Interpretation John Knox 1994

J. Mays Preaching & Teaching The Psalms John Knox 2006

J. Moltmann The Crucified God SCM 1974

B. Pickett The Psalms In Life & Liturgy DLT 2002

O. E. Phillips Exploring The Messianic Psalms
Hebrew Christian Fellowship 1967

K. Schaefer Psalms Studies In Hebrew Narrative & Poetry
Liturgical Press 2001

C. Spurgeon Psalms Vol 1 Crossway 1993

C. Spurgeon Psalms Vol 2 Crossway 1993

C. Spurgeon Treasury Of David Vol 2 Zondervan 1968

R. Harn & B. Strawn Editors Psalms For Preaching Eerdmans 2009

M. E. Tate Psalms 51-100 Word 1990

D. Tidball The Cross IVP 2003

A. Weiser The Psalms John Knox 1962

M. Wilcock Psalms 1-72 IVP 2001

M. Wilcock Psalms 73-150 IVP 2001

T. Wilson The Messianic Psalms Loiseaux Brothers 1978

G. H. Wilson Psalms Vol 1 Zondervan 2002